Also by Wynton Marsalis

To a Young Jazz Musician: Letters from the Road (with Selwyn Seyfu Hinds)

Jazz ABZ: An A to Z Collection of Jazz Portraits (with Phil Schaap;
  illustrations by Paul Rogers)

Jazz in the Bittersweet Blues of Life (with Carl Vigeland)

Marsalis on Music

Sweet Swing Blues on the Road (with Frank Stewart)

Also by Geoffrey C. Ward

The War: An Intimate History, 1941–1945

Unforgivable Blackness: The Rise and Fall of Jack Johnson

Mark Twain (with Dayton Duncan)

Jazz: A History of America's Music

*Not for Ourselves Alone: The Story of Elizabeth Cady Stanton and
  Susan B. Anthony* (with Ken Burns)

The Year of the Tiger (with Michael Nichols)

The West: An Illustrated History

*Closest Companion: The Unknown Story of the Intimate Friendship
  Between Franklin D. Roosevelt and Margaret Suckley*

Baseball: An Illustrated History

*Tiger-Wallahs: Encounters with the Men Who Tried to Save the
  Greatest of the Great Cats* (with Diane Raines Ward)

American Originals: The Private Worlds of Some Singular Men and Women

The Civil War: An Illustrated History (with Ric and Ken Burns)

A First-Class Temperament: The Emergence of Franklin Roosevelt

Before the Trumpet: Young Franklin Roosevelt, 1882–1905

The Maharajas

MOVING TO HIGHER GROUND

Entertaining ourselves during a break in a recording session: me, Victor Goines, Herlin Riley, Wycliffe Gordon, and Eric "Top Professor" Lewis. As the bass player Reginald Veal likes to say, "We don't need no music."

MOVING TO
HIGHER GROUND

*How Jazz Can
Change Your Life*

WYNTON MARSALIS

with Geoffrey C. Ward

 RANDOM HOUSE

TRADE PAPERBACKS

NEW YORK

2009 Random House Trade Paperback Edition

Copyright © 2008 by Wynton Marsalis Enterprises

Published in the United States by Random House Trade Paperbacks,
an imprint of The Random House Publishing Group,
a division of Random House, Inc., New York.

RANDOM HOUSE TRADE PAPERBACKS and colophon
are trademarks of Random House, Inc.

Originally published in hardcover in the United States by Random House,
an imprint of The Random House Publishing Group,
a division of Random House, Inc., in 2008.

Excerpt from an interview with Wynton Marsalis, Artistic Director of Jazz at
Lincoln Center, and Sandra Day O'Connor, former Associate Justice of the
Supreme Court of the United States. This interview took place as part of
Jazz at Lincoln Center's "Let Freedom Swing: A Celebration of America"
performance at the Kennedy Center in Washington, D.C., on January 19, 2009,
and was funded by The Rockefeller Foundation.

Photograph on page 168 by Michael Tran/Wired Images. Photograph on page 183 by Matt
Anderson. All other interior photographs by Frank Stewart © Jazz at Lincoln Center.

LIBRARY OF CONGRESS CATALOGING-IN-PUBLICATION DATA
Marsalis, Wynton
    Moving to higher ground : how jazz can change your life /
Wynton Marsalis with Geoffrey C. Ward.
        p.   cm.
    ISBN 978-0-8129-6908-5
    1. Jazz—Analysis, appreciation. I. Ward, Geoffrey C. II. Title.
    ML3506.M34 2008
    781.65'117—dc22   2008016560

Printed in the United States of America

www.atrandom.com

9 8 7 6 5 4 3 2

Book design by Dana Leigh Blanchette

For Diane

Contents

Passing it on: Piano prodigy Wynton Kelly Guess receives hands-on instruction from Kwame Coleman (behind the pillar) and Eric Lewis. The great drummer Herlin Riley (second from right) is like my older brother. We both played with Danny Barker in New Orleans. I've worked with Eric Lewis and tenor saxophonist Walter Blanding (second from left) since they were teenagers. The other onlookers are proud papa André Guess (left) and our road manager, Raymond "Big Boss" Murphy, who for more than twenty years has made it possible for us to make gig after gig, all across the country.

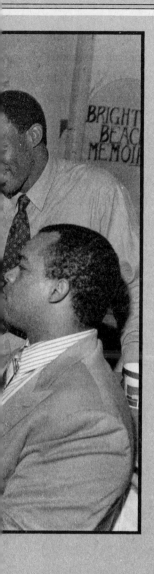

Introduction

"Now, That's Jazz"

In the early 1970s, in the wake of the civil rights movement, when James Brown, Marvin Gaye, and Stevie Wonder were the kings of Afro-American popular music, when people sported eight-inch afros and polyester leisure suits, when the scent of revolution still rode the wind, the last thing anyone hip was thinking about was handkerchief-head, Uncle Tommin', shufflin' and scratchin', grinning-for-tourists Dixieland music. Just the name alone made you hate it. So when my father said he was taking me and my brother Branford to play in a band for kids led by Danny

Barker, the legendary banjo and guitar player, all we could envision was cartoon music or some type of old-school obsequiousness. What was a banjo, anyway? Something they played for Frederick Douglass? Man, we're gonna miss running around on Saturday to go back to slavery days. Yay!

Actually, Danny Barker had played banjo and guitar with everybody from Louis Armstrong and Sidney Bechet to James P. Johnson and Cab Calloway, but we didn't know who any of those people were. We were living in Kenner, Louisiana, at the time. Branford was nine. I was eight. It took my father about half an hour to drive us into New Orleans, to the empty lot where Mr. Barker's Fairview Baptist Church Brass Band was rehearsing.

There we met an old man whom I presumed to be Mr. Barker. He was a colorful character, full of fire and stories well told. He loved New Orleans music and he loved kids. That day, he taught us the most profound lesson about playing jazz—and about the possibility of a life of self-expression and mutual respect—that I've ever encountered.

He started with the drums: "The bass drum and the cymbal are the key to the whole thing. We play in four. One, two, three, four. The bass drum plays on one and three and the cymbal on two and four. It's like they answer each other. So when the bass drum goes *bummp*, you answer with the cymbal—*chhh*."

```
   1        2        3        4
bummp, chhh, bummp, chhh
   1        2           3           4
bummp, chhh, bah-bummp bummp
                        chhh
```

"Now, on that second fourth beat, the cymbal and the bass drum agree with each other. And when you hit them two at the same time, now, that's jazz.

"You see," he explained, "you gotta bounce around with your parts and you gotta skip the rhythm, just like you're dancing."

Then he went to the tuba. "Now, the tuba, that's the biggest instrument out here. You play big notes and leave space. Big things move slow." He sang some tuba lines. "You are related to the bass drum. The two of y'all are down there, so you got to stay with each other. Y'all are the floor—the foundation of the beat."

The tuba player started playing. Mr. Barker said, "You got to play with feeling. And when you play with feeling, on the bottom, you bounce." So he started bouncing. Then the tuba and the drums started playing around. And he said, "You gotta mix it up *and* you gotta play together!" Then, after they made some low, grumbling noise, he said, "Now, that's jazz."

Then he turned to the trombone. "What do you have that nobody else has?"

"The slide," the boy said.

"That's right. In jazz, you always hold up the thing that makes you different from other people. Be proud of being you. You play a low instrument. The lower you go, the slower the rhythms get. So I want you to play this kind of part." And he sang the part. "Every now and then, *rrrhhhhhrrrraawwmmmp*, I want you to slide up, *rip* up, to a note. Tear it up." The tuba, drums, and trombone started playing together and sounded terrible. But Mr. Barker said, "That's jazz music!"

Then he addressed the trumpet players. He said, "Now, the trumpet is the lead instrument. You got to be strong. You play the melody." So he taught us a melody, "Li'l Liza Jane." We started playing. And after we'd played the melody and inflicted a few painful injuries, he said, "Play the notes with personality. Shake 'em! Play around with 'em. And play with rhythm. You've got to bounce, too." Everything he wanted us to do he sang first. So we played the song with everyone else and it sounded like noise. Yeah, it definitely sounded terrible, but it seemed like it might eventually be some kind of fun.

Then he went to the clarinet player. "Now, you see all these keys y'all got. You can play fast, play high, higher than a trumpet; you can play fast skips and trills and such. That makes you different from these trumpet players. I want y'all to do those things every now and then. Play the same melody as the trumpet but up one octave." He sang the clarinet part, too. The clarinet players squeaked and squawked. Mr. Barker listened. Then he said, "Everything you do, you got to do with personality. Scoop and bend and slide those notes." They tried to do that.

Mr. Barker said, "That's jazz! Now, let's hear clarinets and trumpets on the melody. But when y'all play together, you got to talk to one another. The clarinet has to fill when the trumpet leaves space, and the trumpet needs to leave that space." So we tried to play together. The clarinet played the melody up an octave, adding some fast notes but still squeaking and squawking. Terrible. Then Mr. Barker said, "Let's put it all together, 'Li'l Liza Jane.'" It was the most cacophonous, disjointed thing you ever heard in your life.

"Gentlemen," he enthusiastically concluded, "now, that's jazz."

If you look at the New Orleans jazz scene today, a lot of the best musicians—Lucien Barbarin (trombone), Shannon Powell (drums), Michael White (clarinet), Gregg Stafford (cornet), Herlin Riley (trumpet at that time, drums now)—all played with Danny Barker's Fairview Baptist Church Brass Band over the years. So he was hearing something in us way back then. And he was teaching us something, too: You are creative, whoever you are. Respect your own creativity *and* respect the creativity and creative space of other people.

That was the first of many life lessons I've learned from jazz. We hear many things about jazz music these days: that it's only for connoisseurs and too difficult for most people to understand; that it has no identifiable fundamentals or objectives; that the best of it was played in the past in sparsely attended smoky clubs; and finally, that jazz itself is on the undertaker's table, one step from the cemetery.

I've spent the last thirty years doing my best to demonstrate that these observations are just downright wrong. In this book I hope to deliver the positive message of America's greatest music: how great musicians demonstrate a mutual respect and trust on the bandstand that can alter your outlook on the world and enrich every aspect of your life—from individual creativity and personal relationships to the way you conduct business and understand what it means to be a global citizen in the most modern sense.

Most activities that require a participating audience have a way of teaching the newcomer what he or she needs to know to best enjoy what's going on. Sporting events have announcers who interpret the action. Opera has helpful program notes or subtitles. Museums provide audio guides. In jazz, even for musicians, it's generally been "play what you feel," "keep listening and you'll hear it . . . one day," or some other bit of cryptic advice that doesn't inform you but does make you feel unhip. "If you have to ask, you'll never know." That's partly why the aesthetics of jazz remain a mystery to most people, even though the history of its greatest practitioners, from Louis Armstrong to Thelonious Monk to Marcus Roberts, shows that all of them shared the same artistic objectives, which I'll explain more fully as we go along: swinging, playing blues, syncopating diverse material, composing new forms, improvising interactively, exhibiting home-spun virtuosity—all aimed at interpreting the sweep and scope of modern life through the language of jazz.

I'd like to demystify listening to jazz and show you how the underlying ideas of this music can change your life. I'd like to help you feel the music and understand the differences between the sounds and personalities of the great musicians: Dizzy Gillespie, Billie Holiday, Miles Davis, Ornette Coleman, Charlie Parker, Jelly Roll Morton, John Lewis, and more. I'll give you a glimpse of what goes on in the minds of musicians as we play, demonstrate the centrality of the blues, explain why jazz improvisation is different from all other forms of musical improvisation, and explore the creative tension between self-expression and self-sacrifice in jazz, a tension that is at the heart of swinging, in music and in life.

Along the way, I want to pass on some of the lessons the music has given me through the years, lessons about art and life that I hope will help you find—or hold on to—the proper balance between your right to express yourself and have things your own way, your responsibility to respect others while working with them toward a common goal. That's what Danny Barker taught us to do—to enjoy ourselves and one another. And through this music I hope you will be able to do that, too.

Wynton Marsalis

MOVING TO HIGHER GROUND

The closer you get to people, the more they love it: Yet another concert ends with the musicians surrounded by people stomping and clapping and cheering and wishing the swing would never end.

CHAPTER ONE

Discovering the Joy of Swinging

Kids were supposed to stay in the back room. But some kind of way I stumbled into the front room of this tiny wood-frame house in Little Farms, Louisiana. I must have been four or five years old at the time, but I remember it was dark in there, lit only by a soft blue light or a red one, and a lot of grown-ups, men and women, were snapping their fingers on two and four and grooving to a rhythm and blues song. Some sang the words, but they were *all* dancing up a healthy sweat. I didn't know what was going on back then, but I could tell it was something good—so good I wasn't supposed to be around it.

Well, I could be *around* the music, couldn't miss it, actually. R&B was always on the radio: "Baby this" and "Baby that"; "I need you, girl"; "Why'd you leave me? Come back. Ohhh!" That music was a way of life. Everybody knew those songs and everybody loved them: "I Heard It Through the Grapevine"; "Stop! In the Name of Love"; "Lean on Me"; "Papa's Got a Brand New Bag."

Now, jazz was different. That's what my father played: modern jazz. No one danced to it, ever. That had something to do with rhythm. The backbeat of R&B was steady and unchanging. The rhythms my daddy and his friends played were ever changing and many, a torrent of ideas that came together and felt good. I later came to know it as *swing*.

The first jazz gigs I remember going to with my older brother Branford were like recitals. Only a handful of older people turned up. Some gave us candy, and there was always a good opportunity for us to run around. I noticed that very few black people seemed to like this kind of music. As a matter of fact, so few people understood it, I wondered why my father and his friends bothered to play it at all.

Then, when I was about eight or nine, I began to notice something very strange. Even though most of the people in our community would never attend a jazz concert (or anything artistic, for that matter), even though they didn't even consider playing music to be a profession, they had a type of respect for my father. I figured it had to have something to do with jazz, because he certainly was not in possession of any material goods indicative of even the slightest financial success.

I began to pay closer attention to all the jazzmen who came to our house or played with my father in clubs around New Orleans. They were an interesting group, if you could get past how different they seemed to be. First, they had their own language, calling one another "cats," calling jobs "gigs" and instruments "axes," peppering their conversations with all types of colorful, pungent words and unapologetic truisms.

Even if you were a child, they spoke directly to you and might actually listen to what you had to say.

Of course, they talked about men and women, politics and race and sports. But above all, they loved to talk about jazz music, its present and its past at once, like it was all now: "'Trane and them was playin' so much music I couldn't move. And people had been telling me all week they weren't playing nothin'. Man, the music stood me up at the door."

They could go on and on about what different musicians played or did or said, great men who all seemed to have colorful names: "Frog," "Rabbit," "Sweets." It seemed to me that all of these people knew one another or at least had some type of connection. For all of that hard, profane talk, there was an unusual type of gentleness in the way they treated one another. Always a hug upon greeting and—from even the most venerated musicians—sometimes a kiss on the cheek. A natural ease with those teetering on the edge of sanity. A way of admonishing but not alienating those who might have drug problems. Always the feeling that things in our country, in our culture, in our souls, in the world, would get better. And beyond that, the feeling that this mysterious music would someday help people see how things fit together: segregation and integration, men and women, the political process, even the stock market.

That's why these were still confident, optimistic men. Even though they were broke and misunderstood, sometimes difficult of personality, sometimes impaired by a too intense encounter with mind-altering substances and trapped in a culture that was rapidly moving away from professional levels of musicianship, romantic expression, and the arts in general, they still believed in the value of this jazz they played and still understood that their job was inventing music—and making sense of it with one another.

They improvised.

Now, the ability to improvise—to make up things that could get you out of a tight spot—well, everyone needed to know how to do that, even if it was just coming up with the right words at the right time. I thought there must be something to this improvised music. I needed to learn more about it. And hanging around jazz musicians was a great education for a nine- or ten-year-old because they told great stories *and* they knew how to listen. That was their way, talking and listening, listening and talking.

My father could talk for hours, still can. But he would also listen intently and never respond in that patronizing way that drives kids crazy. I have all kinds of memories of telling him partially fabricated stories of what I had done in a football or basketball game and him just standing there listening intently to every detail and cosigning, "Uh-huh. Yep." When he and other jazzmen listened to records or the radio, they could hear all kinds of things I didn't come close to noticing. I couldn't understand how three notes from a tenor saxophone was all they needed to conclude, "That's Gene Ammons," "Yeah, that's 'Jug,' " or "Monk, I hear you, Thelonious!" That seemingly magical ability to hear made me figure that perhaps my father knew when I was embellishing stuff.

He and his friends seemed to be able to follow every moment of what the person played. Now, you have to remember, the rest of us were listening to three-minute records of tunes with words, words that were as easy to memorize as the thirty seconds of repeated musical accompaniment. But these guys were listening to things like Sonny Rollins's "Alfie's Theme," seven or eight minutes of somebody playing all kind of saxophone up and down the horn, following it as if it were spoken by the oracle at Delphi, saying, "Tell your story," and so on. There would be certain points in the music where the "um-hmms" became "ohhh" or "oowee!"—the type of ecstatic eruptions that overcome some people in church. They would respond to Sonny as if he were right there in the room, and during all that seven or eight minutes *not one word* on the recording, spoken or sung! And I'd be sitting there listening to them speak in what was almost a foreign language, trying to understand, wanting to learn it.

At twelve, I began listening to John Coltrane, Clifford Brown, Miles Davis, and Freddie Hubbard. Just by paying serious attention to these musicians every day, I came to realize that each musician opens a chamber in the very center of his being and expresses that center in the uniqueness of his sound. The sound of a master musician is as personalized and distinct as the sound of a person's voice. After that basic realization, I focused on *what* they were communicating through music—pure truth, delivered with the intimacy of friends revealing some secret, sensitive detail about themselves. It takes courage and trust to share things. Many times the act of revelation brings someone closer to you. In learning about a person, you learn something about the world and about yourself, and if you can handle what you learn, you can get closer, much closer to them.

That's why, I came to understand, the scuffling jazzmen around my father were so self-assured. They didn't mind you knowing who they were. With Coltrane, of course, I was impressed with his virtuosity, his ability to run up and down his horn. Everyone who heard him was. But I noticed that the most meaningful phrases were almost never technically challenging. They were succinct phrases that would run right through you, the way profound nuggets from Shakespeare's plays can both cut through you and linger; all those words in *Hamlet*, but you remember "To be or not to be" or "to sleep perchance to dream." Something in those types of phrases reveals universal truth.

The best way I can describe this is by comparing it to the feeling between two people. Before any words are spoken, before one makes any gesture toward the other, there is a *feeling*. And that feeling loses intensity and purity when translated into words or gestures. When someone reaches up to kiss you or says, "I love you," those acts are reductions of that bigger feeling. But if someone figures out how to communicate that big feeling—how to master a moment of soul—he or she just looks at you with directness and honesty and love. Eyes alone can warm your entire body. We most often experience this unencumbered feeling from children. But some adults give it, too. Because jazz musicians improvise under the pressure of time, what's inside comes out pure. It's like being pressed to answer a question before you have a chance to get your lie straight. The first thought is usually the truth.

That purity of feeling is what I heard in Coltrane's sound. His sound *was* his feeling. You also heard Tommy Flanagan's feeling when he improvised at his piano; then you had Paul Chambers's feeling on the bass and Art Taylor's on the drums. A single performance was an improvised symphony of their combined feeling, made more honest by the pressure of time.

It's not easy to find words for the kind of emotions that jazz musicians convey. You don't have a name for the feeling of light peeking through the drapes in your childhood bedroom. Or how the teasing by classmates hurts. You don't have a name for the feeling of late-night silence on a car ride with your father or how you love your wife's smile when you tease her. But those feelings are real, even more real because you can't express them in words. Jazz allows the musician to instantly communicate exactly how he or she experiences life as it is felt, and the instant honesty of that revelation shocks listeners into sharing and experiencing that feeling, too.

Some popular music evokes nostalgia. Your memory of your own emotions fills the songs with meaning: "You remember this one, baby? This was when I had that old beat-up Oldsmobile and used to pick you up in it and this was our prom song." But jazz music is about the power of *now*. There is no script. It's conversation. The emotion is given to you by musicians as they make split-second decisions to fulfill what they feel the moment requires. The explanation can be complicated, but the music is very direct and basic. And because Coltrane felt so strongly about things, his sound remains potent and present. We can still feel him and Louis Armstrong and Thelonious Monk and all of the great ones. And we can feel and empathize with many other musicians, too, if we allow their sounds to reach and fill some space inside of us.

Jazz makes it possible for individuals to shape a language out of their feeling and use that very personal language to communicate exactly how the world feels to them. Recordings froze the sounds of these musicians, affording us the pleasure of entering their world whenever we wish. The world according to Lester Young. Mmmm. That's where I want to be. Then, to be there over and over again.

The best jazz for me back then, however, was always live. I loved to hear my father and James Black or Clark Terry or Sonny Stitt electrify a room. Live, the music unfolded right in front of you. All over you.

Now, at first I could hear and relate to 'Trane's sound but didn't necessarily understand what he was playing. It was hard to follow. One solo had enough music for about forty of the radio songs that I could comprehend. But I kept trying to hear and follow, like a kid listening to adult conversation.

Then, one day, I could actually understand—not in my mind but in my heart. It came to me all of a sudden. What he was playing made perfect sense, actually super-sense. These musicians were telling stories. And these bittersweet stories unfolded in unpredictable ways. The musicians themselves were often surprised by their inventions. But they worked with the surprises the way a bull rider adjusts his weight and angles to stay onboard. It was a language, and after you could comprehend the song of the language there was no need for words. The song *is* the language. The song *was* the language.

When I started learning about jazz, I wasn't into any kind of art. I had no idea it could have a practical purpose. Now, more than thirty years later, I testify to the power of art, and more specifically jazz, to improve your life—and keep on improving it.

I know now that my father and his fellow musicians possessed such confidence because of their relationship with an art form. Although they struggled with our way of life, with segregation and all types of small unnamed injustices, with personal situations that were as full of drama, unhappiness, and strife as anyone else's, they enjoyed who they were.

I noticed that religion gave some people a way to *escape* dealing with the world: "Things will be better when you die," the people of my grandma's generation said as they worked themselves to death. "God wants you to forgive and love those who do you wrong," some people said to shake off the shame of being unable to respond to the abuse they endured. The holier-than-thou faction found comfort in believing, "The rest of y'all are lost because you don't have a personal relationship with God—*our* God."

But art engages you *in* the world, not just the world around you but the big world, and not just the big world of Tokyo and Sydney and Johannesburg, but the bigger world of ideas and concepts and feelings of history and humanity.

I learned that jazz has the power to help anyone willing to engage it. Some people think music communicates only when it accompanies lyrics—that's why pop music almost always has words. But as in all art, whether we encounter a great play or poem or painting, artists can carry us to a common place: When they cry, we cry; when they are excited, we become excited. And jazz music, because it is mostly wordless, allows musicians to express deeper, more varied, and ever changing states of being. It can provide musicians and listeners alike with a sense of self, a concept of romance, a more comfortable physicality, a deeper understanding of other human beings. It is an endless road of discovery leading to more maturity and acceptance of personal responsibility, a greater respect for cultures around the world, an invigorating playfulness, an excitement about change, and an appetite for the unpredictable. It gives you a historical perspective, a spiritual acceptance of necessary opposites, an undying optimism born of the blues—and a pile of good listening.

I went through my teen years playing all kinds of music. But jazz became my real love. I grew up with it and wanted to be able to play it. This was the 1970s, when most of what we thought of as jazz was some funk tunes with horns playing the melody. But my exposure to real jazz musicians at an early age helped me realize that this music had a different function from the pop music we loved and played. The most popular music of my youth thrilled people with illusion, sentimentality, and showmanship. Music was just one of the tools we employed to create excitement. The jazzman's objective, however, was solely musical: Through his improvisation, he wanted to take people deep into his actual feelings and his world.

Ironically, I was in the same position Bix Beiderbecke found himself in when he first heard jazz music as a teenager in Davenport, Iowa, in 1917. Most of the people around him thought jazz was some kind of hokum, a gimmicky fad that—to make matters worse—was created by black people who weren't worth anything, anyway. But through intense listening, Bix could hear past all that ignorance and racism and learn to hear the differences among black groups, white hokum groups, and white groups like the New Orleans Rhythm Kings, who could really play. He could recognize artistic objectives, too, and set out to become an artist himself, even though pursuing those objectives would drive him farther and farther away from the world in which he grew up.

Like Beiderbecke, I wanted to figure out what separated jazz from what we were being *told* was jazz.

What is jazz really saying?

Is it still of value?

This is some of what I found.

The most prized possession in this music is your own unique sound. Through sound, jazz leads you to the core of yourself and says

"Express *that*." Through jazz, we learn that people are never all one way. Each musician has strengths and weaknesses. We enjoy hearing musicians struggle with their parts, and if we go one step further and learn to accept the strong and weak parts of people around us and of ourselves, life comes at us much more easily. A judge has a hard time out here.

Miles Davis, for example, couldn't play with the big sound of Louis Armstrong, but he found his own type of intensity at a softer volume. He would release recordings with mistakes, and they still sound good. The imperfections give the music even more flavor and personality. In this era of young people starving themselves to attain some Madison Avenue or TV version of thinness and perfection, the idea of "working with what you have" provides a more useful alternative.

Jazz also reminds you that you can work things out with other people. It's hard, but it can be done. When a group of people try to invent something together, there's bound to be a lot of conflict. Jazz urges you to accept the decisions of others. Sometimes you lead, sometimes you follow—but you can't give up, no matter what. It is the art of negotiating change with style. The aim of every performance is to make something out of whatever happens—to make something together and *be* together.

Back then, these two revelations—*the importance of expressing the core of your unique feelings* and *the willingness to work things out with others*—gave me more than I needed to address the increasingly complex personal relationships that can be unbearable for a teenager. On a basic level, this music led me to a deeper respect for myself. In order to improvise something meaningful, I had to find and express whatever I had inside of me worth sharing with other people. But at the same time it led me to a new awareness of others, because my freedom of expression was directly linked to the freedom of others on the bandstand. I had something to say, and so did they. *The freer they were, the freer I could be, and vice versa.* To be heard demanded that we also listened to one another. Closely. And to sound good we had to trust one another.

Of course, I'm talking especially about the benefits of playing, but it goes for listeners, too. The value of jazz is the same for listeners and players alike because the music, in its connection to feelings, personal uniqueness, and improvising together, provides solutions to basic problems of living. Deeper levels of listening yield even more benefits. As in conversation, a musician knows when people are listening—and inspired listening makes for inspired playing.

Knowing jazz music adds another dimension to your historical perspective. I have read about the Great Depression, and I knew and played with people who lived through it. But when you listen to Mildred Bailey or Billie Holiday, Benny Goodman's orchestra or Ella Fitzgerald with the Chick Webb orchestra, you gain insight into those eras: the language they used; how they employed humor and stereotypes to bridge the gulf between ethnicities; their conception of romance as reflected in the interactive grooves they danced to; how sweet, hot, and Latin music came together. You can *hear* that people were figuring out a way to celebrate and define their existence joyously in spite of—and to spite—the hard times. Not just with happy tunes but with the verve and downright swing—the jubilant back-and-forth rhythm—that jazz musicians brought to every kind of tune, even songs of pathos and loss. Jazz fills the dry facts of American history with something sticky and sweet.

Jazz music is America's past and its potential, summed up and sanctified and accessible to anybody who learns to listen to, feel, and understand it. The music can connect us to our earlier selves and to our better selves-to-come. It can remind us of where we fit on the time line of human achievement, an ultimate value of art.

The greatest artists in any field speak across epochs about universal themes—death, love, jealousy, revenge, greed, youth, growing old—fundamentals of the human experience that never really change. Art and artists truly make us the "family of man," and most of the greatest jazz musicians embody that consciousness. Entering the world of jazz gives you an opportunity to commune with brilliant creative thinkers—Max Roach and Gil Evans, Papa Jo Jones and Mary Lou Williams, and many, many more—and, through the workings of so many diverse minds, demonstrates that there are countless viable ways to improvise—to think through the same problems and deal with them. Some musicians, like Coleman Hawkins, take things apart and reassemble them, piece by piece. Others, like alto saxophonist Paul Desmond, play with clear, dry wit. You might wonder how a musician can be witty. A witty person turns a familiar phrase in a quick and humorous direction; a musician can do the same thing with melodic phrases: You think you know where the next phrase will go, but it goes somewhere else with the timing and power of a good punch line.

With jazz, there are as many approaches as there are people who can play. Musicians like Bix Beiderbecke, Miles Davis, and Booker Little focus their intelligence and feelings on creating deep, haunting, heartbroken sounds. Charlie Parker expands our concept of the mind with quickness of thought and mastery of organization at incredible tempi.

Louis Armstrong, more than anyone else, figured out how to use the hard-earned realism of the blues to toughen up the sentimental, pie-in-the-sky corniness of many American popular songs. In the process, pop was infused with Afro-American rhythm and artistic elevation through the art of improvisation, and jazz gained a body of superbly crafted melodies and sophisticated harmonies.

European composers frequently used folk themes, the popular music of their day, as points of departure for fantasies and freewheeling compositions that utilized all kinds of complex compositional techniques, from fugue to serialism.

The jazz musician, on the other hand, almost always maintained the rhythm and harmonic structure of the melody when improvising. From traditional fiddlers' reels and church music to the blues and the nineteenth-century cornet soloists who performed spectacular variations on popular themes like "The Carnival of Venice," most improvising in American music has followed a theme-and-variations pattern.

Louis Armstrong inherited all of these traditions. He improvised not only on the melody and harmonies of popular songs but on their sentiments as well, taking us through spontaneous ruminations on a startling range of human responses to the idea of romance, from heartbreak to absurd humor to excruciating tenderness. He showed jazz musicians all around the world how to improvise on the most universal of human themes, what Duke Ellington called "the world's greatest duet, a man and a woman going steady."

American standards—the best-loved popular songs of the 1920s, '30s, and '40s—became the framework for the jazz musician to build on, rich source material covering almost every known circumstance, from adolescent gullibility to middle-aged apathy to dysfunction in old age. Jazz musicians have such respect for these songs that the great tenor saxophonist Ben Webster once stopped in the middle of his instrumental improvisation because he "forgot the words."

With jazz, affairs of the heart are open to many interpretations. And because all you have to do is learn an instrument and some harmonies, and because you can invent your own compendium of late-night vibratos and effects, and because the pressure of time forces you to be spontaneous, and because intimacy and honesty are more practical than formality and convention, and because you don't have to learn composition and orchestration—and because of the absolute realism and hard-won joy of the blues—jazz musicians get closer to expressing the actual diversity in the ways of love than any musicians before them. There is the transcendent sensuality of Johnny Hodges, the super-sensitive secrecy of Miles Davis, the distanced but expert elegance of Duke Ellington, the acerbic sweetness of Stan Getz, the playful sexuality of Harry "Sweets" Edison, the heartbroken laments of Billie Holiday. Each of these musicians—and many more—gives you a tour of the sweet ups and downs of romance. Their discoveries can give you the confidence to step into your own feelings, to recognize the uniqueness of your partner's feelings and let them unfold, to revel in those soft moments and not be afraid of the silences that can make them even softer.

Jazz is the art of timing. It teaches you *when*. When to start, when to wait, when to step it up, and when to take your time—indispensable tools for making someone else happy.

Time is the lifeblood of jazz. Not the time told by a clock or even the time signature on a piece of music. *Swing* time: the quality of the quarter notes played by the bass down low and the cymbal up high as they shuffle through a song. ("Frère Jacques" is made up of quarter notes; replace the words with *doom* and you'll be singing a swinging bass line.) The triplet-based shuffle rhythm invites all kinds of dynamic figurations on the piano and horns. (If you want to know what a triplet is, think of any Irish jig.) Everyone dances, and the bass and drums hold it all together. They are like the man and woman in a family, two extremes of register and volume coming together. The quality of their negotiation affects the quality of the time. If they get along, things go smoothly. If they don't, you have a lot of interesting stories to tell.

My father and his friends had just two questions about a new musician: "Can he play?" meaning, "Does he have good ideas and a distinctive tone?" and "How's his time?" meaning, "Does he create a good-time groove with his rhythm?" Jazz can teach us how to be *in* time. There are always three kinds of time at play when you're on the bandstand: actual time (the dry, relentless passing of seconds and minutes), your time (how the passage of actual time feels to you), and swing time (how you adjust your time to make actual time become *our* time).

Actual time is a constant. Your time is a perception. Swing time is a collective action. Everyone in jazz is trying to create a more flexible alternative to actual time. Bass and drums become the foundation of swing time, and the rest of the band interprets the swing from their rhythmic viewpoint. Some rush, some slow down, some play right on the beat. But all shift back and forth, trying to find and maintain some common ground. You're in time when your actions are perceptive and flexible enough to flow inside that ultimate constant—swing.

Being in time has many practical applications outside of jazz. Swing is a matter of manners. When you are in time you know when to be quiet, when to assert yourself, and how to master the moment with an appropriate or unusually inventive response. Fast-thinking comedians can do that. So can athletes who make intelligent decisions that involve teamwork even though the pressure of the clock makes them want to do something solitary and, generally, stupid. To be in time requires you to make the subtlest kinds of adjustments and concessions to keep everyone in a groove. And your colleagues have to be willing to do the same for you. In most bands, it is the subject of intense discussion:

"Man, you're dragging."

"You rushin', Rasputin."

"What kind of time are y'all playing? Can you just give me some good time to play on?"

"Call me back when y'all are ready to swing."

"Can you hear what we're doing up here! Please, man, stop lagging and join us."

Bass players and drummers argue constantly about the time. Generally, bass players rush and drummers drag. So, there's almost always conflict in the kitchen. The rhythm guitarist once served as the referee, but he unfortunately faded from the rhythm section when the big bands stopped being commercially viable. But that rhythm guitarist is the most self-sacrificing of musicians, willing to do less than he or she might do so that others can do more. The rhythm guitar is by far the softest instrument but also the most central. It plays every beat as if to remind us, "Here's home." When everything is right, the rhythm section's like a trampoline: Stiff but springy, it lets everyone else jump around and have a great time. Too stiff or too soggy, and we have a bad time.

Science says the only constant is change. But to swing is to alter how we experience that change. The musician's relationship to time can be of ultimate assistance to you in: 1) adjusting to changes without losing your equilibrium; 2) mastering moments of crisis with clear thinking; 3) living in the moment and accepting reality instead of trying to force everyone to do things your way; 4) concentrating on a collective goal even when your conception of the collective doesn't dominate; 5) knowing how and when to expend your individual energy.

Being in time also gives you the confidence to take chances. The beauty of a musician who sits comfortably in time is the many wondrous rhythms he or she can invent. Sonny Rollins comes most immediately to mind. He scrapes the beat, pushes it, leans on it, makes taffy out of it. He takes chances like a great juggler, an acrobat, or an explorer. He says "Let's see what's over here" or "I bet I could combine this with that and make it work." And it does. He plays super-syncopation—the *unexpected* unexpected rhythm. Thelonious Monk does it, too. It's as if they go deeper into time by floating out of it. And just when you think they're gone—*poom!*—they're back again.

They show us not only how to navigate change but how to initiate it, inspire it, and revel in it. We're often told that time is our enemy, something we can't control. "Time flies!" "Don't waste time!" "Do it while you're young!" We live in a youth-oriented culture where becoming older is treated like a crime. Older people show you pictures of themselves when they were younger, proud of how they *used* to be. Younger people can't be bothered with anything having to do with their parents' time (that's old), let alone their grandparents' (that's ancient).

But in jazz, someone fifteen can be on the bandstand next to an eighty-year-old. I have seen Sweets Edison in his seventies, Roland Hanna in his sixties, and Reginald Veal in his twenties, all chasing the elusive swing with the same zest and vigor. And believe me, many times the old men would be showing the young ones where to put the beat.

In jazz, time is your friend, and when you find your own swing, or the swing time in any group activity, actual time flies, yes. But it's flying to where you want to be. And when you get there, you realize the ride is the destination. That's the joy of swinging.

Call and response: I don't know whether Cassandra Wilson had ever played with Mark O'Connor before, but those initial accompanying phrases from his violin clearly impressed her and inspired her to respond with appreciative surprise.

CHAPTER TWO

Speaking the Language of Jazz

"These damn directions! I think we're lost, man. Don't follow the printouts. Follow what the man gave us."

We've all experienced uncertainty when following directions.

"Did he say left on Bush Street or Bushnell Avenue?"

"Was that an Exxon station or Texaco?"

Sometimes you get lost because of your own inability to follow directions. Other times, it's because a landmark that "everyone around here knows" is only visible to those who saw it when it was actually there. In any case, it's natural to second-guess information when you're not sure where you are and don't know where you're going. But sure enough, if you stick with it, you'll have your "Eureka!" moment.

"Aha! Webster Street."

You know everything is going to be all right. That name—Webster—tells you exactly where you are.

It's the same way with jazz. The music's terminology is like the music itself—direct and plainspoken. It tells you what's going on. Listening becomes more enjoyable when you understand the meaning of a few key terms like "breaks," "riffs," and "call and response."

Jazz musicians have to listen *and* communicate. You have absolutely no idea what the other musicians are going to improvise, so you're forced to listen. And because the accompaniment is improvised, a soloist is required to quickly communicate the logic of what he or she is playing—as quickly and completely as possible. Everyone follows the music as it's being born, requiring each person to listen and speak with the same intensity. That's why much of the terminology of jazz is analogous to verbal communication.

THE SOLO

A solo is an accompanied soliloquy, for example, one person declaring "I am." In the earliest days of jazz, the first two decades of the twentieth century, musicians didn't solo. They would just improvise little melodic embellishments. Then there was a gradual evolution in those embellishments, like the way a child learns to speak. First "mama," "da-da," and "no," then phrases like "I no want to bath," and finally, a sophisticated use of language and connecting of ideas meant to con you into some disagreeable form of sponsorship: "Buy me that toy, please! All my friends have it."

In jazz, short improvisational phrases evolved into much longer melodic excursions, which eventually became chorus after chorus of free-flowing improvisation. For example, if you listen to King Oliver's solo on "Dippermouth Blues," followed by Louis Armstrong's solo on "West End Blues," then Charlie Parker's on "The Funky Blues" and John Coltrane's on "Bessie's Blues," you can get a good sense of how soloing changed, from artist to artist, time period to time period.

I'm not saying that 'Trane's solo is "better" or more "advanced" than Louis Armstrong's, because it's not, but it's certainly longer and reflects a vocabulary that includes ideas drawn from Oliver, Armstrong, and Parker. Armstrong knew what Oliver played, Parker knew what Armstrong played, and Coltrane started playing because of Parker. Each musician communicates with his predecessors, building on some aspect of what they did while contributing something of his own.

The best musicians would put portions of familiar melodies into their solos to give listeners something to hold on to. That made following an extended solo a little like hearing people speak a foreign language that you almost understand. There are three or four phrases you can identify but other words just keep coming and coming. Eventually discouragement overcomes the initial recognition and excitement, but you stick with it because you know that people are communicating concrete ideas. With music, the ideas are invisible—thought, emotion, aspiration—but no less concrete, no less rewarding to understand. Stick with the music, and its meaning will be revealed.

The jazz solo gave a larger number of musicians the opportunity to put their creative imprint upon the history of music. The player was also the composer; the recording, not the score, became the definitive document.

How many great classical virtuosos have been denied their total creative voice because of an inability to compose? Speaking through the voice of a great composer is one thing, but saying your own thing exactly the way you hear it is something else altogether. Jazz was a new thing. If you were willing to improvise and invent a personal way of playing your instrument (not necessarily an easy thing to do), then you only had to learn some chord progressions, some popular melodies, and the blues (which, as we'll see later, is the lifeblood of American music), and you could become a creative jazz musician and put your feeling all through some music—and all over some listeners.

CALL AND RESPONSE

After imitation, the most basic form of communication is call and response. Somebody calls your name, and if you have good manners, you say "Yes?"; if you don't, you say "What?" Jazz musicians love all types of musical call and response: Louis Armstrong's opening trumpet call on "West End Blues"; Count Basie's band responding to the singer Jimmy Rushing on any blues they performed together; and "Mademoiselle Mabry," Miles Davis's response to Jimi Hendrix's "And the Wind Cried Mary."

The early blues recordings of singers like Bessie and Mamie Smith feature the call of a blues lyric and some sort of instrumental response. Bessie Smith's "Young Woman's Blues" is a classic example. The horn player, in this case cornetist Joe Smith, is trying to play with as much expression as the singer and provide more rhythmic and musical sophistication at the same time.

SCAT SINGING

Call and response inspired instrumentalists to play with the freedom and nuance of the human voice, as Ray Nance did on any trumpet solo he ever played with Duke Ellington's orchestra.

(Nance plays the classic solo on "Take the 'A' Train.") It also motivated singers to raise their level of mastery and led to the wordless, improvised emulation of horn players called scat singing: *Ba-da-ba-dee-doo bee-yee-bah-dee doobeeyah*. This stuff is fun to do. Louis Armstrong ("Heebie Jeebies") and Ella Fitzgerald ("Lady Be Good") were masters of scatting. The name *bebop,* the postwar style developed by Dizzy Gillespie and Charlie Parker, comes from the scat-sung sound of their instrumental improvisations. A definitive bebop tune is Dizzy's "Oop Bop Sh'Bam."

VOCALESE

Scat singing, in turn, led to the development of vocalese, putting words to all the notes of celebrated recorded instrumental solos, allowing singers to tell long stories in the language of jazz. An excellent example is Jon Hendricks's vocalized version of one of the best-loved recordings in jazz history, "Freddie Freeloader" from Miles Davis's *Kind of Blue.* It features Bobby McFerrin, Al Jarreau, Mr. Hendricks, and the guitarist George Benson singing lyrics to every note played by Wynton Kelly, Miles, Coltrane, and Julian "Cannonball" Adderley.

Meanwhile, instrumentalists developed ways of scooping and bending notes to sound like talking, laughing, and crying: Listen to Cootie Williams's plunger mute—the business end of a toilet plunger—on Duke Ellington's "Concerto for Cootie" or Joe "Tricky Sam" Nanton's trombone on "Ko-Ko"; the gruff tenderness of Ben Webster's tenor saxophone on a late-night ballad or the inescapable holler of Roy Eldridge's trumpet on something hot like "Let Me Off Uptown," recorded with Gene Krupa and His Orchestra. People were making all kinds of vocal sounds on horns—and those exhortations always produced some kind of response from other musicians and from listeners, too.

Because jazz draws upon everyday human interactions, it demands different techniques than previous forms of Western music do. Gimmicks that impress, the way circus tricks do, are less respected in jazz than techniques that directly and honestly communicate personal emotions and reflect the grandeur and absurdity of being human.

The call and response between the brass section (trumpets and trombones) and the reeds (saxes) is a signature technique of the American jazz orchestra. Count Basie's classic "One O'Clock Jump" is full of calls and responses. So are "Jumpin' at the Woodside," "Taxi War Dance," and "Swinging at the Daisy Chain." I could go on and on—because brass-reed conversation is what Basie's men especially liked to do.

THE SHOUT CHORUS

At the end of a big-band arrangement, the brass section sometimes starts shouting the same thing over and over. Then, here come the reeds responding again and again with a repeated line of their own. This is the shout chorus, and through repetition it can build to an almost unbearable intensity. No shout chorus is more ecstatic than in Bennie Moten's "Blue Room." If that one's not enough for you, try the one in Casa Loma Orchestra's "Casa Loma Stomp." The shout chorus says, "This song is about to end." Dancers and listeners go crazy.

As economics forced the big bands out of business after World War II, there were fewer brass and reed sections engaging in dialogue, so soloists like Lester Young learned how to call and respond all by themselves. They would play an initial call, then respond in the next phrase with other thematic material. This was yet another way to organize ideas in a jazz solo. But no soloist could play all the time. So other instrumentalists began filling the void, such as drummer

Max Roach responding to melodic phrases played by Charlie Parker's saxophone on "Segment" and Herbie Hancock on piano responding to Miles Davis's trumpet on "My Funny Valentine." Eventually, bassist Charles Mingus gave everyone on the bandstand the opportunity to call and respond with tunes like "Moanin'." Virtually every tune played by the Bill Evans Trio was one big call and response.

When listening to any great jazz group, you can hear musicians responding to the call of one another's improvisations with consideration, elegance, and grace. This teaches us how to call, listen, and respond, a progression basic to communication but—because of that word in the middle, "listen"—a balance difficult to achieve in real life.

How many times have we said or heard "I don't think you understand what I'm saying," followed by an overconfident response that demonstrates very clearly "No, I don't"? This unsuccessful call and response happens in music, too—in fact, it happens much of the time. At a concert you struggle through it, but the recordings I'll talk about throughout this book demonstrate how equilibrium can be reached when musicians really listen to one another.

RIFF

Jazz shows us how to find a groove with other people, how to hold on to it, and how to develop it. Sweets Edison, Count Basie's most original and soulful trumpet player, once told me that if a phrase felt good enough, bands in Kansas City might repeat that same phrase over and over for thirty or forty minutes *without stopping*. Musicians and dancers fought to see who could get to the deepest groove and, once there, make it last the longest. Repeated phrases like these are called *riffs*.

At first, a riff meant any imaginative improvised melody. Immediately after his trumpet solo on "Up a Lazy River," Louis Armstrong verbally comments on how good he sounds: "Oh, you dog! Boy, am I riffin' this evening, I hope sump'in'."

Later, riffs came to mean repeated melodic nuggets. Anyone with children knows the proper usage of a riff:

"Sit down in the car."

"Sit down in the car."

"Sit down in the car."

Or:

"Eat your food."

"Eat your food."

Or:

"Stop hitting your sister."

"Stop hitting your sister."

Riffing drives the point home, repeating and building in intensity. It does that in music, too. Good riffs are always compact, meaningful, well balanced, and catchy. They can show us how to speak succinctly, get to the point, and stay there.

Eventually, horn players found another way to use riffs: to signal another horn man that it was time to *stop* soloing. This drove Charlie Parker crazy when he toured with the Jazz at the Philharmonic troupe. His inventive brilliance made some of the other men so insecure that after he'd played one or two blazing choruses they would start blowing solo-ending riffs to keep him from embarrassing them further. (It didn't do much good; he could always show them up on the next tune.)

When discussing the music, we always speak of the best. In reality, much that takes place on bandstands reflects the petty and jealous interactions that all too often, in jazz and in life, prevent a deeper understanding of one another. With jazz, though, the possibility of sounding good makes you strive to be your best self, in order to play better. And Charlie Parker always played better.

BREAK

In the early days of jazz, before solos, a band would sometimes stop for two or four bars, and one person would fill the space with an improvised phrase. This is called a break. It's a pressure-packed moment, because you have to maintain the time flow of the whole band by yourself: Our time becomes *your* time—yours and yours alone. If you mess up the break the entire band will want to kill you, because everyone has been nursing the time flow since the beginning of the tune. There you are, dropping the touchdown pass.

As if to one-up everybody, the young Louis Armstrong actually improvised a harmonic accompaniment to King Oliver's solo breaks. Pops, as Armstrong came to be called, was so familiar with the King's style that all Oliver had to do was signal what he was going to play and Louis would invent a harmony part to it, on the spot. On "Snake Rag" you can hear Armstrong's harmonic mastery and lightning reflexes, gifts that terrified Chicago musicians in the 1920s.

Most breaks are one or two bars long, but Dizzy Gillespie's "A Night in Tunisia" features a *four*-bar break. Four bars is a long time to be out there on your own. All that open space without accompaniment can make you question your own timekeeping abilities even when you have good time, and the slightest doubt can throw your rhythm completely off. To be off even a little bit on a break is to commit a crime against swing.

A great break demonstrates pure grace under pressure. Talk about mastery of the moment! It can show us the value of paying close attention to all aspects of a group's interaction. In a break you can summarize and forward the group's intentions or give a fresh direction to its momentum.

HEAD CHART

Sometimes, you'll see a musician point to his head on the bandstand and suddenly everyone will begin playing the melody. It looks like some mystic signal until you learn that we call the melody the *head*. A head chart is an on-the-spot arrangement of a tune without written parts, just a series of improvised and harmonized riffs, calls and responses, and the melody. (Head charts sometimes get written down and refined into formal arrangements; some of Count Basie's best-loved pieces came about that way.) If you're playing a sad solo, musicians may say, "Play the head, man. Please!" as if to beg you not to subject them to any more pain.

This brings up the matter of bandstand etiquette. When a musician starts playing the head while you're soloing, that's tantamount to saying "Shut up." If the decision to go to the head is premature or based on jealousy or some type of rancor, everyone else can shake it off and continue to play, as if to say, "No, no, keep going." Then, the soloist can and should keep playing. But if everyone joins in playing the head, it really is time to end the solo. Sometimes people with very bad manners keep soloing anyway, but in general musicians accept the checks and balances that govern live performances. It's like something we used to call a "dap-off." When it's time for a conversation to end, one person gives a soul handshake ("dap") to the other. This is supposed to signal "I'm ready to go." But sometimes a person holds on to your hand and keeps talking, even though he's been dapped-off. This is very bad form: The next time you get dapped-off, *be* off.

THE RHYTHM SECTION

We're often told that jazz is the ultimate expression of individual freedom. After all, the most famous musicians are soloists: Miles Davis, Louis Armstrong, Art Tatum. In actuality, the heart of a jazz band is the rhythm section—piano, bass, drums, and sometimes guitar—and their freedom comes through supporting the soloists. They're like the parents in a family: They work while the kids have all the fun. But if that rhythm section isn't right, everyone has a bad time.

I once had a chess set in which the rook was a bass player and the knight was a drummer. Back when my older kids were nine or ten, I always loved to hear them plead, upon losing one of those pieces, "No! Not a member of the rhythm section," because even at that age they understood that a rhythm section is a serious thing.

The rhythm section is purely a jazz invention: three instruments (sometimes four) whose sole job is to make the music feel good.

Rhythm section players must have great reflexes, because they have to improvise and create accompaniment for someone who is making up what he or she is playing on the spot. It's like being expected to anticipate what someone is going to say next and then find the appropriate response to it *while he or she is saying it*.

For a horn player, finding a great rhythm section can be better than finding a great lover. You'll do almost anything to keep them, but most times they don't want to be kept. The average life of a great rhythm section is about five years. The greatest rhythm sections get named and become legendary, like Count Basie's All-American Rhythm Section: Papa Jo Jones, Walter Page, Freddie Green, and Basie himself.

I have noticed certain personal characteristics—stereotypes, really—that seem to define members of a rhythm section. Bass play-ers are generally big and affable. Drummers are usually short and quick-tempered. And piano players are the know-it-alls, the only musicians who can play a three-hour gig all by themselves and feel quite comfortable with it.

With its long and noble history, a piano is an orchestra all by itself. Most great European composers played the piano. Beethoven played it (that's enough to prove my point right there), and a large library of pieces has been composed for it. When people ask what instrument they should get their children to play, the answer is usually the piano. Piano players used to be called "Professor," because they generally understand more about the mechanics of music than the rest of us do. We are always asking them for the proper chord progressions. (That doesn't make us like them more.)

Pianists get around. They play in hotels, restaurants—all over. It's sometimes said that jazz was born in the brothels of New Orleans. While trumpet players were not fortunate enough to get this kind of work, pianists did. They also played in Wild West saloons and middle-class parlors, and felt right at home in the palaces and concert halls of Europe.

Then, in a purely American example of class reversal, the piano, the star of instruments, was put into the role of accompanist—not just for some celebrated singer or great violinist, but for *any* saxo-phone, clarinet, cornet, or even trombone player. This change in fortune demonstrates the attitude adjustment needed to be part of the rhythm section. It's the type of adjustment the American demo-cratic process has been known to give the high and mighty: You may have been a king where you come from, but you're just "John" over here.

The jazz drum kit is really a combination of instruments—drums of various sizes and a whole array of cymbals. Drummers in Western musical traditions are known for making all kinds of racket with trumpet players (except in Scotland, where the drummers play with bag-pipers). In the classical German symphonies of Mozart, Beethoven, and Haydn, kettle drums play with trumpets. Afro-Cuban music is all about drums and trumpet.

In any jazz big band, if you don't have a written part for the drummer, you give him the first trumpet part, because the first trumpet plays most of the accents the drummer must play to lead the band. Drummers are the real conductors of the jazz band. They control the dynamics, the tempo, and the feel. (The master, Papa Jo Jones, did this better than anyone, but Art Blakey was no slouch, either. The first did it with finesse, the second with fire.)

In jazz, the drummer has to forgo the façade of supremacy to be supreme at the core. He or she is required to sacrifice volume for equilibrium and the mindless intensity of bashing for the intelligent intensity of balance. Good drummers serve as sterling examples of how to lead any group, even a family. It's how real leaders are. Teddy Roosevelt said it best: "Speak softly and carry a big stick."

RIDING AND WALKING

In an act of supreme irony, the loudest instrument in jazz—the drum—plays on every beat with the softest instrument—the bass. We call it "two right hands." The right hand of the drummer rides the cymbal with a stick on every beat while the bassist walks the bass by plucking a note on every beat. It's like the relationship many kids observe between parents. One carries the stick, the other carries the sugar. Over the years, just as the price of things has gone up and up, drummers have played louder and louder, changing the fundamental relationship of drums to the band and opening the door for all kinds of acts of poor citizenship.

When bass players started using electric amplifiers to defend themselves against loud drummers, one of the most fundamental checks and balances in jazz was altered. The softest instrument became one of the loudest instruments—if not *the loudest*—and was set free to wreak havoc. And it does. This failure in the kitchen has led to some of the worst home life in jazz. That's why a drummer like Lewis Nash is always in such demand. He plays with a subtlety and control that invites bass players to participate because they can be heard without straining.

The bass is a rhythmic partner of the drums. It also shares harmonic duties with the piano, providing bottom notes to its cycle of harmonies. The bass can also function melodically when responding to a soloist, playing countermelodies or soloing itself.

In jazz, we should probably give the bass more melodic passages. One of the great achievements in European music is melodic freedom in the bass. From figured bass continuo parts, which are functional and many times nonmelodic, to romantic symphonies in which the bass interacts with the rest of the orchestra, a rich dialogue between higher and lower parts has been fostered and developed to create a more melodically diverse music.

A VAMP

In jazz, the bass is caught between worlds: Should it play what we call a *vamp*, repeating the same handful of notes over and over again? Or should it play quarter-note swing? Or should it interact with the melody—or do all three? When the bass and drums depart from their interlocking rhythmic pattern, the band is less likely to swing or groove—but the music becomes more intricate and conversational. It's all a matter of choices and expectations.

Most popular music today is vamp-based. The bass and drums repeat the same two- or four-bar phrase for the duration of the song. This repetitive groove is infectious and easy for dancers to follow.

With jazz, the bass moves around *and* grooves, and the swinging interaction of bass and drums leads dancers into a dynamic relationship with one another and with the music. Because Americans didn't hold on to swing as the national dance, youngsters took to the simpler, mindlessly repetitive, booty-shaking grooves we still love today. Since the advent of the twist, fewer and fewer people have experienced the romantic interplay of swinging, Lindy Hop couple dancing.

THE GUITAR

Let's not leave the rhythm section without talking about the guitar. You almost never hear it in a modern rhythm section. (The great composer and pianist John Lewis used to tell me all the time to add the guitar to our big band, because it adds rhythmic clarity to the swing.)

As time passed, drummers got tired of sacrificing volume and then bass players got sick of not being heard and turned up their amplifiers. Well, as I said earlier, the guitar was once the *most* altruistic instrument in a rhythm section. Softer than the bass, playing on all four beats of a measure with bass and drums, and articulating the harmony with the piano, the guitar was almost never really heard, only felt. But once rock and roll put the guitar front and center and turned up that volume, who in the world was willing to choose being felt over being worshipped?

As jazz evolved, the rhythm section became more aggressive. The modern rhythm section darts in and out of the background, creating a more fluid relationship with the soloists and often matching wits with them directly. The great rhythm sections of the 1960s—those that played with John Coltrane, Charles Mingus, Miles Davis, Ornette Coleman, Thelonious Monk, Art Blakey, and the Modern Jazz Quartet, for example—made this rapid-fire call and response *the* way to play. Each rhythm section has a distinctive style and approach to solo accompaniment and the art of swinging. Today these two fundamental responsibilities have been undermined by drum and bass solos on nearly every tune. Many times nowadays, bassists are waiting to solo instead of concentrating on swinging.

TRADING

Before the era of five-minute bass solos, when only the greatest of bass players soloed at all, drummers would occasionally get climactic solo spots and a few breaks. Then, starting in the 1950s, the solo order evolved. Generally the leader, say saxophonist Charlie Parker, would solo first, then the second horn and other horns, then the piano, and then, if God willed it, instead of a full-blown drum solo the soloists would alternate phrases with the drummer. This is called *trading*.

Eventually, the bass began soloing after the piano. Pretty soon, songs lost all shape and logic, becoming vehicles for everyone to solo till he got his fill. No wonder many audiences get bored.

The failure of this solo-based form teaches us that sometimes it's better for everyone *not* to have his say on every tune. In any case, the exchange with drums is called trading fours, eights, twos, or ones, for that matter. (We almost always alternate even numbers of bars because they are easier to count and feel.) This provides an opportunity for real one-upmanship and later leads to much heated discussion about who "got" who.

Simply saying "fours" or "eights" on a bandstand means you want to trade with the drummer. As a horn player, you'd better be on your toes, because drummers brag a lot if they out-rhythm you—even though they don't have any harmonic or melodic responsibilities.

JAM SESSION

It's late, say 12:30 or 1 A.M. You have found some way to get to a place somewhere in the world where people swing till all hours of the morning. The room has a bandstand. The walls are hung with pictures of jazz musicians throughout history. Sometimes the place is packed, sometimes not. Sometimes it's run-down, sometimes fancy. You go to the bandstand, shake everyone's hand. They call a tune, perhaps "Have You Met Miss Jones?" and *wooosh* . . . there you go. People start smiling and cosigning—shouting their approval of what's being played. Some musicians are happy, others sad. The bartender starts sending drinks up. You are at a jam session. Cats with horns come out of the woodwork. If the rhythm section is right, you might stay there and play, or just listen, soaked in swing, until the sun comes up.

CUTTING SESSION

Every now and then, someone with bad intentions climbs onto the bandstand and you find yourself in a battle of music. Whenever you outdo someone else it is said you have "cut his head." That's why this is called a *cutting session:* Someone will get cut and go home with hurt feelings. It's not that he doesn't deserve it. Maybe he has been talking about how you can't play and now he's going to prove it. He comes in blaring loud and fast and high. Uh-oh! Overly technical displays impress musicians but after a while leave audiences staring at some undefined point in space. To distinguish yourself you have to play something *different*, not just loud, high, or fast. You've got to float and croon and whisper. The faster someone plays, the more predictable the rhythm becomes. Keep an opponent off balance with unpredictable but swinging rhythms and you might just go home happy.

SWINGING

We all hear a lot about how jazz and improvisation go hand in hand. It's true: Improvisation is the most enjoyable part of jazz for any musician, and collective improvisation is cathartic when it goes right. But many kinds of music feature improvisation successfully. What makes jazz improvisation unique? The most obvious difference is rhythm. Jazz swings—or at least it's supposed to be trying to swing.

As with other wonderful human activities, swinging is a matter of equilibrium, of balance, of knowing when, how, and how much. It's the irresistible distillation of the European march and waltz and the African 6/8 into a four-beat dance rhythm of remarkable elegance, roundness, and grace. (You may not know what the African 6/8 is but you've heard it; it's normally played on a cowbell and has six beats per cycle.)

Our current lack of respect for the swing can be likened to the current state of our democracy. Balance is required to maintain something as delicate as democracy, a subtle understanding of how your power can be magnified through joining with and sharing the power of another person. When that is no longer understood, it becomes a battle to see who is the strongest, who is the loudest, who can get the most attention.

The strong are free to prey on the weak.

That's what happened to the swing. Drummers started happily drowning out bass players. Bass players fought back with their amps. Piano players began playing short, choppy rhythms to battle with the snare drum. The rhythm guitarists gave up and went home. The horn players just went crazy and soloed all night long on one tune. The result was perfect *im*balance, freedom of expression without concern for the whole. Though many have accepted this unswinging approach, I'm sure that one day musicians will assess the damage, and all over the world we will see a return, in jazz, to the swing.

Technically, swinging is the feeling of accented triplets in 4/4 time. You probably know "The Mickey Mouse Club March." It's a great example of swinging because it's built on a shuffle rhythm, which is the basis of swing.

Now it's time to say good-bye to   all our com-pa-ny

The basic beat is counted 1, 2, 3, 4. Now, if we subdivide each beat into three and accent the third part of each beat, it becomes a shuffle: 1 2 *3*, 2 2 *3*, 3 2 *3*, 4 2 *3*. That accented 3 is hard to control, but it gives a musician tremendous rhythmic flexibility.

To understand this chart, start with the basic beat and the melody as expressed through the words. After working that out, notice that the syllables that are accented align with the faster rhythm at the bottom.

Basic Beat	1		2		3		4			1		2		3		4	
Triplet Subdivision	1	2	3	2	2	3	3	2	3	4	2	3	1	2	3	2	2	3	3	2	3	4	2	3

Basic Beat	1		2		3		4			1		2		3		4	
Shuffle (accented 3rd beat)	1	2	3´	2	2	3´	3	2	3´	4	2	3´	1	2	3´	2	2	3´	3	2	3´	4	2	3´

Basic Beat	1		2		3		4			1		2		3		4	
Shuffle	1	2	3´	2	2	3´	3	2	3´	4	2	3´	1	2	3´	2	2	3´	3	2	3´	4	2	3´

Now's it's time to say good-bye to all our com-pa-ny

In music, rhythm is almost always connected to dance, and the dance is often the centerpiece of cultural rituals and rites of passage. Swing—the dance and the music—bespeaks the flexible nature of American life. In jazz, the bass walks a note on every beat. The drummer rides the cymbal or plays brushes on every beat. And everybody else invents melodies and sounds that sway with, against, and upside every beat. Every beat requires musicians to reassess their relationship to one another. This is what makes swinging so challenging. You are forced to be constantly aware of other people's feelings. The art of swinging can be reduced to "be together." And it's hard to accomplish. That's why bass players and drummers argue all the time. No one person can control the ebb and flow.

Swing demands three things. It requires extreme coordination, because it is a dance with other people who are inventing steps as they go. It requires intelligent decision making, because what's best for you is not necessarily best for the group or for the moment. And it requires good intentions, because you have to trust that you and the other musicians are equally interested in making great music and are not guided by ego or musical shortcomings that haven't been addressed.

And you don't have much time! Swing is a thought-reflex. When swinging, the time passes so quickly you can't rethink your original instinct; you have to go with what you feel is the right thing. Swing tests your inner resources; it can make you question who you are, make you reach deeper, make you respond more freely. When musicians swing, they are doing in music what we would like to do when we speak: say exactly what we feel so that our fellow conversationalists understand and accept it and are moved to reveal in response what *they* know and feel.

The swing is also a great listener. It cosigns and amens you and leads you deeper into what you want to say. And here is the sweetest part: It does that for everyone, whether he or she is playing or dancing or listening.

The loss of swing is the great tragedy of American popular dance. It led us away from couples dancing. I don't mean they stopped dancing together entirely, but swinging made you want to investigate the nuance of your physical relationship with your partner. Nowadays, in clubs, that happens only occasionally on slow songs—if there are any.

We need to bring swing back, not out of dumb, misguided nostalgia but because swing is a modern rhythm, much more suited to the increasingly integrated world of today than anything pounded out by a drum machine and recorded by people who are not even in the same studio together. "E-mail me my part and I'll record it and send it back to you and you can mix it into the recording. Through the marvels of modern technology, I never even have to see you."

When a band is truly swinging, the musicians, the audience, and even—sometimes—the critics pat their feet, nod their heads, and shake a proverbial tailbone in absolute recognition. There are other aspects of jazz, however, that are mainly the domain of musicians. Technical discourse is not a common occurrence in jazz writing, because, in the immortal words of Duke Ellington, "that type of talk stinks up the place." You can't discuss jazz, however, without saying at least a little bit about form.

FORM AND HARMONY

People ask me all the time, "Are you just making that stuff up?" The answer is "Yes, we are making it up, but it is made up in the context of a repeating form." Especially the thirty-two-bar song form.

Now, of course, not every piece of jazz employs a repeating form, but many do. If you want to perceive the form, start by counting. Songs like "Honeysuckle Rose," "What Is This Thing Called Love?," "You Don't Know What Love Is," and "Take the 'A' Train" all have a form that is thirty-two bars long. Those bars can once again be counted 1 2 3 4/2 2 3 4/3 2 3 4/4 2 3 4, and so on, and are divided into four sections of eight bars each:

```
 A      A      B      A
[ 8 ]  [ 8 ]  [ 8 ]  [ 8 ]
```

As you can see, three of the four sections have the same thematic material. The third one is different—it is called the *bridge*.

"Oh, Lady Be Good" is perfect for learning the thirty-two-bar form. After the first eight bars are repeated we come to the bridge. You can count through it if you want to, but take the time to notice that the melody changes and so does another element—the harmony.

This starts to seem complicated if you think too much about it. But some people think dancing to music is difficult, too, and instead of moving in time, they start thinking about where to put their feet, on what beat, and then the hips, then the head. Meanwhile the music is going on and on, and they end up embarrassed and standing by the wall. It's much easier to just get out there and start doing what you can. You'll get it. Many, many people have. Explaining dancing is much more difficult than doing it. Harmony is damn near impossible to explain but easy to hear and feel.

I remember my father telling me that when he began playing piano gigs, he noticed that songs changed keys at some point. He further peeped that the key change happened at a regular interval, which he later learned was the bridge. Once he connected the bridge to the rest of the song, he said, he could play on the A A B A form of most standards.

Miles Davis's "So What" is a great song to teach you about bridges, because it has only two harmonies: the harmony of the A section (D minor) and the bridge (E-flat minor). Going up one-half step from D to E-flat presents a harmonic contrast that's easy to hear.

Leonard Bernstein once told me that harmony and harmonic progressions were the hardest musical concepts to explain to non-musicians. Jazz musicians call a progression of harmonies *changes*, meaning chord changes. When I was a kid my father and his friends, after greeting one another, would invariably ask, "How's your old lady?" Many times the response was, "Running me through some changes." That meant they were having a hard time.

In jazz, harmonic changes force you into different musical environments. Each harmony contains a set of notes from which you construct improvised melodies. This set of notes is called a scale. The changing harmonies involve different scales. To be successful, you must be able to hear how harmonies relate to each other and be able to articulate melodies that successfully navigate these relationships as they change.

When I was nineteen or so, Wayne Shorter told me, "Notes are like people. You have to go up and greet each one." Well, I thought he was crazy. But now I understand what he was saying. You have a relationship to notes, scales, and chords, and the more intimate that relationship is, the richer the music you make.

There are as many approaches to harmony as there are people. Furthermore, two people will relate to each other in one way, which changes when you introduce a third. Adding a fourth may ruin the vibe, and so on. Harmonies are like that. You may be great with the first six or so, but that seventh chord kills your solo. You can be very technical and scale-oriented about harmony or you can find pungent blues melodies that cut through harmonic barriers and still sound good. It's like playing tennis: You might be great on grass but terrible on clay and mediocre on asphalt. Now, imagine eighty other surfaces and you will understand why the so-called avant-garde movement that started in the early fifties and still sees itself as the cutting edge was so eager to consider playing through harmonies old-fashioned and obsolete.

Some time ago, the tenor saxophonist Frank Foster was playing a street concert from the Jazzmobile in Harlem. He called for a blues in B-flat. A young tenor player began to play "out" from the first chorus, playing sounds that had no relationship to the harmonic progression or rhythmic setting.

Foster stopped him.

"What are you doing?"

"Just playing what I feel."

"Well, feel something in B-flat, motherfucker."

CHORUS

When jazz musicians improvise, they create new melodies that fit within a bar structure that repeats over and over again. Most often, as I've explained, it's thirty-two bars. But the form could be eight bars like Coltrane's "Resolution" from *A Love Supreme*, twelve bars like Charlie Parker's "Now's the Time," or even sixteen like Monk's "Light Blue." Whatever the number of bars, one cycle is called a chorus, and in a three-minute performance there may be ten choruses. What happens in choruses delineates an arrangement the way décor distinguishes cubicles in an office space. Everyone's cubicle has the same amount of space; every chorus has the same number of bars. Each person decorates his or her space with a different personality and intent; every chorus contains a different idea or color or flavor, unless a soloist runs out of ideas or goes on too long—or a bass player solos at any length. (Tenor saxophonists sometimes like to unburden themselves like that, too.)

Now, we've gone over a lot of the terms that will help you find your way into jazz. What I've left out is the blues. The blues is so central to jazz music that it needs a chapter all its own.

The blues can be found anywhere: Here's Joe Temperley, the most soulful thing to come out of Scotland since the bagpipes, calling the children home—in Holland.

CHAPTER THREE

Everybody's Music: The Blues

I have played with all types of musicians in every type of setting, from Pooh's Pub to City Park to an ancient Roman amphitheater to the Sydney Opera House, and with everybody from B. B. King to Itzhak Perlman, Sonny Rollins to Willie Nelson, and Stevie Wonder to the masterful flamenco guitarist Paco de Lucía. I'm talking about impromptu performances, without rehearsal time or organized music. What sorts of songs could all these diverse musicians possibly find to play together under those circumstances? What do all have in common?

The blues. It's as if the blues was born to give us an excuse to play with one another, to understand one another. When in doubt, reach for the blues. It'll be there.

We played a gig in Turkey once, and a guy came onstage with some Turkish instrument we couldn't even identify. He asked what we could play together. From the look of his instrument, our first answer was "Nothing." But after he shook off a few songs, we said, "What about some blues?" A big smile came over his face and he said, "Of course." He fit right in, and the people loved it because they could hear their traditional music and our music together in a digestible form. I played just the other day with some cats in a New Jersey state penitentiary. What do you think we played? Mainly the blues. They were swinging, too.

With the blues you have layers of meaning. The words say one thing, the way they're sung can say another, and the music always says something else. For all of the sorrow of some blues lyrics, the music is always grooving; a groove implies dance, and dance always brings joy. Dizzy Gillespie said it best: "Dancing never made nobody cry." That's the key to understanding blues. The blues delivers both joy and sorrow.

The blues is a great preacher. She's going to explain the underlying nature of things. She's determined to get to you, through exhortation, appeal, explanation—whatever it takes. The blues musician does the same thing with his instrument, crying or moaning, shouting or whispering—anything to provide the healing you need.

The blues is a vaccine: It's the controlled dose of something bad that prepares someone to deal with the approaching uncontrollable bad. It's the way some parents acted in slavery times, treating their kids harshly to arm them for what was coming. Or the way the military abuses new recruits to prepare them for the rigors of combat.

Sweets Edison told me the blues was the saddest sound you ever heard. Joe Williams said the same thing. Horace Silver said it was the most joyous sound. So did Clark Terry. It's perfectly designed to give form to what we feel at any time.

Technically, the blues form is a twelve-measure cycle that is repeated over and over for the duration of a song, just as the hands of a clock go around and around all day long. This form features three harmonies like the beginning, the middle, and the end of things. Three sung statements and three instrumental responses. The Holy Trinity. The blues.

Here are some traditional blues lyrics:

Went down the hill, put my head on the railroad track.
Went down the hill, put my head on the railroad track.
When that train come runnin', I snatched my fool head back.

This chart provides the formal layout of a typical twelve-bar blues.

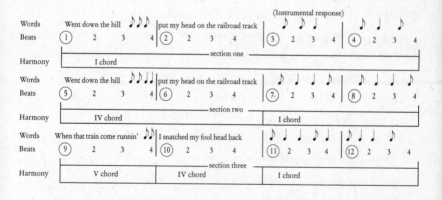

The chart may look complicated, but if you understand a couple of basic concepts it's easy to grasp. We count months by days; each month has roughly thirty days. We count measures with beats; a typical measure of the blues has four beats. The earth moves through seasons as the months pass; there are roughly three months for each of the four seasons, equaling twelve months per year. In the same way, the blues passes through harmonies as the measures change; there are three harmonies divided into three sections—one harmony in the first, two harmonies in the second, and three harmonies in the third—each of the three sections has four measures, equaling twelve measures per one chorus of blues.

When my son Jasper was born, he came out crying and gasping for air. The nurses snatched him up, cleaned him off, stuck a tube up his nose to clean his nasal passages, pricked his foot to take blood, and roughly poked and prodded every area that you wouldn't want to have poked and prodded. Welcome! Whew! Then, finally, they gave him back to his mama and she hugged all over him. Pain and love. That's the blues, right there.

The blues smacks your behind *and* cradles you. It's hard to explain with words, but once you hear what's there, you realize it's what you felt all along.

The blues is you crying over something, wailing, actually. *And* it's about your coming back. That's why the blues is such a good sound track for life. It covers the extremes of experience without being fussy or self-pitying, and it promises better times to come. That ultimate optimism runs right through the entire history of the blues in jazz: W. C. Handy's "St. Louis Blues" to Jelly Roll Morton's "Dead Man's Blues" to Count Basie's "Good Mornin' Blues" to Charlie Parker's "Now's the Time" to Ornette Coleman's "Ramblin' " to Duke Ellington's "Blues in Orbit."

Leon Wieseltier told me the blues should be our national anthem because so much of the best American music is based on the blues. I agree. But the blues recognizes no national boundaries. There is a whole genre of tunes called Japanese blues. The Chinese opera is full of blues-like themes. I could go on and on, because the sound of the blues can be found in much of the world's music.

The moans and cries, humorous asides and embarrassing outbursts that give character to human expression regardless of language—the blues.

The pentatonic scales of Eastern music and the three fundamental harmonies (chords) of Western music called one, four, and five—the blues.

A twelve-measure structure like the twelve months of the year or the twelve signs of the zodiac—the blues.

The major and minor sounds derived from the Greek modes when sounded at the same time or played in contrast to one another—the blues.

The amen cadence in Christian church music—the blues.

The bent notes and melismatic singing of Indian and Middle Eastern music, the pungent timbre and intonation of some African music, the deep gypsy flamenco cries of *cante jondo* in Spain, church hymns, nasty whorehouse songs, the singing of workmen in the field and on the levees, Broadway show tunes, the work of classical composers like Darius Milhaud, Aaron Copeland, and Igor Stravinsky, who wanted to put some "more American" in their pieces, even theme songs for cartoons like *Spider-Man*—what do you think? The blues.

Some people have tried to trace the blues to Africa. Well, maybe blues are from there, but *the* blues is from America. All the technical musical elements came together here, and because there was more personal freedom here, people were much more relaxed about telling you exactly what they felt about the pain and pleasure of life, romance, sex, and love. Remember that many of the original blues people didn't enjoy all of the American liberties, so the "freedom" part of their song was delivered with the type of gusto always exhibited by the denied whenever they participate in what has been withheld. That's why the early blues people loved talking about getting away, escaping.

W. C. Handy, a preacher's son, was trying to escape the shackles of the church. Mississippi bluesmen tried to catch that freedom train up north, away from segregation and the legacy of slavery. The early

Blues Queens tried to break away from the stereotypical passive roles of women by celebrating freedom from some type of unsuccessful love. (Ida Cox was talking about this when she sang "Wild Women Don't Have the Blues.")

The blues gets all inside of you because it's filled with tragicomic reality about life and love and pain and death and stupidity and grace. It's about *what is*—and what is has demons and angels sitting right at the same table. When Son House sings, "I never knew how much I loved her, till they laid her six feet down," he's saying, "I found the depth of my feeling in this loss." W. C. Handy's "Aunt Hagar's Blues" is about a pious churchwoman who can't resist the blues. "If the devil brought it," she says, "then the good Lord sent it right on down here to me." In other words, "These blues might seem evil but the Lord knows we need them down here." Yes.

The blues trains you for life's hurdles with a heavy dose of realism. John Philip Sousa's music is stirring. It's national music of great significance. But Sousa's is a vision of transcendent American greatness: We are the good guys from sea to shining sea. The blues says that we are not always good. Or bad. We just *are*.

You're born with the blues and you die with it. That's why it seems timeless. A researcher once asked the New Orleans clarinetist "Big Eye" Louis Nelson just when the blues began. "Ain't no first blues," Nelson answered. "The blues *always* been." And though the blues is most often about men and women and the things we like to do together, it can be about anything—a flood (Bessie Smith's "Backwater Blues"), empty pockets (Smith's "Poor Man Blues"), or a mean boss (something Max Roach and Abbey Lincoln spoke about with "Driva Man" from *We Insist! Max Roach's the Freedom Now Suite*). Bluesmen and -women improvise their stories. Sad or funny, factual or fantasized, raunchy, majestic, or even maudlin, the blues reassures us with the unpredictable inevitability of life itself. Bad as things may be, they will get better or they could have been worse, and no times are so bad they can't be turned into good times. Just consult Ray Charles's "Let the Good Times Roll" and you'll know why the blues will never die.

That uncrushable optimism is part of what makes the blues so American. Triumph is our forte. American art doesn't end up in cataclysm like Wagner's *Die Götterdämmerung*. At the end of our movies, the boy gets the girl and all the people we thought to be dead are still miraculously alive. We prefer happy endings. The blues promises: "Everything gon' be alright this mornin'," and perhaps, to some, that worldview might seem naïve. But there's nothing naïve or superficial about the blues. Oh, no. The blues, in all its incarnations, *begins* with pain.

I've always played some form of blues. You couldn't help it if you lived in New Orleans. One of the first songs I learned at eight years old was a blues, Joe Avery's "Second Line." In high school I played with a funk band, and even after a night of big-afro-platform-shoe-backbeat, we would still play "Second Line." That was our birthright, our Crescent City tradition. But the actual depth of expression of the blues was not something we considered—and we never heard anybody play who made us consider it. Or if we did, our tastes were so shaped by the popular music we played, danced to, and listened to, we wouldn't have recognized it. We didn't listen *into* music, we listened *at* music. We wouldn't have recognized any meaning beyond the words. So when we played the blues it was largely devoid of meaning—and no one we played for would have recognized that meaning even if it was there. Blues and jazz musicians were at the bottom of the food chain then; their recordings weren't on the charts, their music wasn't new, and the girls didn't like it, at all.

Because many tourists came to town to hear "old-fashioned" music and because so many older musicians defiantly clung to their heritage, there was more blues music in New Orleans than in any other place. But we were still Americans: We assigned value by how much money could be made, and at fourteen, playing in a funk band, I could make much more per night at dances than blues- and jazzmen made in clubs. Therefore, we never, ever considered the aesthetic significance of blues—or any other non-money-making music, for that matter.

A few of us respected jazzmen like John Coltrane, because we were still musicians, after all. But we didn't understand the importance of the blues element in his playing. We could hear the depth of feeling in his sound, but we didn't connect it to the blues. What really impressed us was how he played through chord changes. Speed, fire, and volume—that's what mattered in the 1970s, when people were playing so loud that just to be heard required an act of God. Light shows, dance steps, and background vocals were much more important to the success of our gigs than any coherent musical improvisation. Solos were not meant to say anything; they were meant to excite the crowd. It made you feel like you were in the circus, except for the girls. They let you know it was a gig. And you didn't have any problem with that.

It's ironic that only after I left New Orleans at seventeen and moved to New York did I begin to understand that there was a blues aesthetic and that it was already a part of my experience. I owe that understanding to two people.

The first was the writer (and cutting-edge drummer) Stanley Crouch. I met him during my first New York winter at a thoroughly swinging neighborhood club on West Ninety-seventh Street and Columbus Avenue called Mikell's. He introduced himself to me, but I was already aware of him because my father had followed a heated exchange of ideas in *The Village Voice* between him and Amiri Baraka about something involving the police. In my father's estimation, Crouch had taken the high road in his response, whereas Baraka had seemed upset and unprofessional. That said a lot to me, because my father respected Baraka. Crouch and I began talking back and forth, trading insults. He started by telling me I couldn't play and I told him something about his head. (In New Orleans we played the dozens all the time, rhyming about the size of somebody's head or lips or something—but not about his mama. That's new. I loved the dozens, but if you talked about somebody's mama when I was growing up you would get your ass whipped. Definitely.)

Crouch invited me to come to his place in the Village to talk about music. I didn't know many people in New York, so that was a big social event for me. His girlfriend, Sally Helgesen, cooked a great dinner, and it felt like being back home. Crouch had books and records everywhere, and he began talking about Duke Ellington and Ornette Coleman and all kinds of musicians I'd never really listened to but had all kinds of opinions about. It was almost surreal, this guy who could play the dozens sitting in this room surrounded with so much material, thinking and writing so deeply about all of this stuff, having such concern for the meaning of things. It was mind-boggling, actually. I was not hostile to thinking or to the verbal exposition of thoughts, because my father and mother were both into education and books and conversation. But Crouch was so passionate and informed about so many topics—including jazz—that developing a friendship with him was like going to a school you couldn't wait to get to. Even after all these years we remain very close. Whatever differences of opinion we may occasionally have, the respect and love I have for him will always be deep and unqualified.

Crouch told me I had to meet the writer and cultural critic Albert Murray. Now, that was truly a revelation. This was the late seventies, early eighties. Malcolm X's ghost was riding the wind, and Black Nationalism was the chosen philosophy of every young black person of consciousness. I was full of anger and the fire of youth because I had grown up in small Louisiana towns that were immersed in a prejudice that had been refined over centuries. My generation had been taught that things were going to be different, and in a lot of ways they were, but there was still a lot of bullshit in the air that you were expected to put up with.

Even though this was not long after the civil rights movement, for us the fifties and sixties already seemed like a long time ago. Older people didn't talk that much about how segregation had affected them, and more than a few aspects of American life were *still* segregated. Many of my generation considered older black people to be Uncle Toms and handkerchief-heads if they didn't talk some type of Black Nationalist rhetoric.

Of course, we had a very limited knowledge of American history and almost no understanding of recent Afro-American history, even though we were living in its shadow. We didn't know where we were on the time line of our country's life or where we belonged in physical space. We were lost—and still are. We thought older black people were victims of circumstance who put up with all kinds of stuff we were not about to tolerate—riding in the back of buses (even though we still rode in the back by inbred habit), deferring to white folks' intelligence all the time, and just general ass-kissing and bootlicking. To us, the blues was part of that. It represented what we were trying to get away from: somebody moaning about his woman to hide the reality of white people's foot stuck up his behind.

We used to say a tune was "just" a blues. We didn't understand that there was so much of value in the Afro-American tradition, so much to help us survive our contemporary struggles. We didn't realize that the blues was a handy tool if you knew how to use it, and we couldn't imagine that the blues could provide you with a sense of pride and of belonging. We were caught between the twin pillars of an inadequate educational system and a debilitating but highly successful marketing campaign to exploit the so-called generation gap. Those things kept you ignorant and happy. We didn't think about them; that's just how it was—and still is. And the millions of victims are out here right now, older and influencing what's happening by blindly living the lies and misinformation we were all taught.

Many of my non-Afro-American friends want to know why black

Americans don't support the blues or jazz or anything of quality from their own culture. It's not that we don't like it; actually, we love it—we just don't know that we love it. The collective conclusion we came to after the civil rights movement—the *unconscious* collective conclusion—threw the meat out with the fat, let the blues go the way of the Negro leagues. But with the blues there were no "major leagues" to go to. The blues *was* the major leagues.

Nowadays, the average black person has *no* idea, *no* understanding of the rich legacy of the Afro-American arts and doesn't know that there is even something to know. Common knowledge has led us right back to the minstrel show by way of rap music and corrupted church music to the point of people hip-humping while singing about Jesus. This is sad for black people and even sadder for our country, because black Americans occupy a central position in our national identity.

When Crouch and I stepped into Mr. Murray's apartment on 132nd Street, it looked like a scene from a movie. All kinds of books and records but—unlike Crouch's—all organized. Romare Bearden and Norman Lewis paintings on the wall. A lot of stuff neatly crammed into a small place. At first, I didn't understand what Mr. Murray was talking about. He presupposed a lot of knowledge I wasn't close to having. But I was impressed by how much he knew about a diversity of subjects and how they were all related.

Most black intellectual conversation I had experienced centered around black and white—black *versus* white. Not Mr. Murray's. He loved to talk about Louis Armstrong and Duke Ellington (I, in the typical fashion of a young black would-be revolutionary, was unfamiliar with their music), but he would talk with just as much enthusiasm and insight about Faulkner, Yeats, and Thomas Mann. He didn't differentiate between men by race. He dealt with the quality of their ideas.

Nothing in my background had prepared me for that. The jazz

musicians I'd known were all extremely intelligent, but they were a breed apart from the rest of the world. The education I received in school avoided the intellectual achievements of black folks altogether. Here was a man who had been in the military and was a college graduate and was from two or three generations before mine and was as far from a handkerchief-head as you could get. And here he was, sitting up in some Harlem apartment in obscurity, surrounded by fifty years of collected books and recordings of the most meaningful ideas in the history of humanity, and he was asking you to pull down this book and that one and go to chapter so-and-so and page so-and-so, and on that *exact* page would be what he was talking about, and it was everything from Plato to John Ford to Frederick Douglass to thermonuclear dynamics to James Brown; and his wife, Mozelle, reminded you of all the best, most loving people in your family; and he was excited about you, that you wanted to learn about something, and *he* told you the blues was the truth, and gave you a book he wrote about it, and you took it home and read it, and it was full of stuff you had experienced your whole life but had never considered important or special, but now you knew that its specialness was based in its universality and that the idea of reducing the blues aesthetic to race was impoverished, and now, because you had actually felt exactly that before he told you, him telling you was like a cue from a conductor: You know when to come in, but his cue makes you doubly secure; it guides you to where you were going anyway, and now it's going to take much less time and things won't feel the same because you're not alone. You have help. Plenty of it.

Mr. Murray's *Stomping the Blues* was the first book I ever read that dealt with aesthetic objectives around music and life as I knew them. To this day, I've never read anything like it.

But playing the blues is different from reading about them, no matter how provocative the ideas. All of the study you do in books, all the knowledge you can gather about music or human behavior, will not help you play if you don't have the ability. Any of us who once aspired to be athletes and did not make it had to face at some point the fact that hard work may not be enough. Ultimately, no one knows what enables a person to play or to have any talent, for that matter. But with the blues, as with other aspects of any art, knowledge only augments your ability; ignorance does not enable talent.

That's where playing is different from listening. If you try to listen you will achieve success. Anyone can enjoy a great performance if he or she is willing to invest the time to understand what success means in that art form. In high school, I always hated reading poems with a lot of symbolism: "Why can't they just tell us what they mean?" But once I realized how the symbolism enriches the poem and allows you to get more information with fewer words, I began actually enjoying the skillful use of symbols.

The blues is full of metaphor in words and music. If you don't believe me, check out Alberta Hunter's "Kitchen Man" and you'll see what I mean. Informed listening leads to enjoyment.

It's a lot like reading. If you don't want to follow a plot or look up words or learn about anything, at your own pace, literature is probably not for you. But if you do, there's a whole untapped world and a lifetime of discovery and enjoyment waiting for you. With the blues and jazz, a little bit of investment will yield a multitude of emotions, all kinds of spiritual riches—and just a damned good time.

I once asked the great John Lewis how he defined jazz. He said, "It has to swing or seem to swing. It has to contain the element of surprise, and it has to embody the eternal search for the blues."

Well, you don't have to search far to find it. Country and western has its version of blues. So do bluegrass and funk. R&B is the blues and so is rock and roll.

Some people think playing blues has to do with whether or not you suffer from some obvious social pathology. Man, everyone on earth pays some kind of dues. With the blues, the question is, How did those dues hit you? What do you want to do about it? How do you want to make other people feel? And do you have the courage and ability to tell them about it? If you want to get rid of your blues and do the same for other people, playing the blues is the best way I know to do it.

There's something strangely personal about how you play the blues. It's impossible to imitate another person's blues feeling. You can learn some runs or licks, but you can't find the same sound. No two people play the blues alike. Someone can sound like John Coltrane but not on the blues. Especially when it's played slow. The slower a blues is, the less you can imitate and the more you are forced to find your own holler, your cry, your thing. That makes the blues musician easy to identify. A listener can hear the difference between artists by the way they play the blues.

When I first got to New York the older musicians had no respect for what I played. Virtuosity? Yes. Substance? No. One night Ray Brown and Milt Jackson called me up on the bandstand. I was eighteen or so and playing all fast. So what do you think they put on me? Slow, slow blues. I mean *slow*. What could I do? I went into super-fast runs, hit some high notes, repeated one thing over and over again, circular-breathed, exhausted the whole lexicon of things we did in my generation to get applause. Most of the people in the club that night knew what jazz was supposed to sound like, so I didn't get the type of house I was accustomed to getting. Still, I hoped my playing didn't sound as sad as I knew it was. All hope of that was shattered when Milt asked me, "You notice the difference between how it sounded before you came up there and after you came up there?"

I said, "Yeah, I heard that."

"You know what the difference was?"

"What?"

"You wasn't up there!"

And he was right, too. It's hard but it's fair. I had not yet learned to put my own personality and feelings into how I played. I had just begun to understand that the blues could help you focus your passion and intelligence. I was still coming from the "It's just the blues" philosophy. That experience led me to reevaluate my playing and emphasize substance and honesty over pyrotechnics and sentimentality.

Another night, Sweets Edison did the same thing to me. He called a slow blues. "Man," Sweets said when I was done, "you just played more notes than I played in my entire career." Implied in that was "And you didn't say anything."

I said, "Let's see you handle some of these complicated songs *we* play."

"I'll just play some blues through all that confused shit," he answered, "and make it sound like music."

All the older guys would mess with me in those days: "What you playing, Flash?" "We playing some blues up here, Fly-by-Night, why don't you come and join us?"

I finally figured, "Why not? They're playing it and sound damn good. They must know. Generation gap or not, I'm going to take a chance on their knowing what they're talking about."

I have learned that the biggest mistake a jazz musician can make is to run from the blues. In my septet we had a saying about the type of self-knowledge that scares you: "Don't run from it, run toward it." And the blues can be found anywhere. That's what John Lewis meant when he talked about the eternal search for the blues. It's also why, when you embrace the blues, no matter who you are, you're embracing your own heritage as a human being.

"I've never heard anyone your size get such a big sound": Jazz for Young People concert at Jazz at Lincoln Center.

CHAPTER FOUR

*What It Takes—and How It Feels—
to Play*

Jazz teaches empathy—you create and nurture a feeling with other people—and it also teaches you to do your own thing. In our music, there are so many ways for people to find and express their individuality, no single set of rules could possibly apply.

When I was growing up, I noticed that jazz musicians loved all kinds of strange people who would be outcasts in any other setting. It seemed like there was room for everybody—and even more room if he or she could really play. I was fascinated by how different types of people figured out their own way to improvise. Sometimes a person had perfect pitch or knew intuitively how to play what fit, whereas other people had to use scientific methods to figure out what scales would work with the harmonies of songs. Others had no dexterity whatsoever, but could play with a particular depth of feeling and apply the blues to whatever they played. They had what was called "a personal sound."

One musician might not have been able to hear harmony that well but had a good sense of melody. Still another might have had a good sense of rhythm but no melodic ability. He had to stick to two or three notes and hope things worked out. In any case, everybody understood that *nobody* had everything, so it was best to embrace what people could play and to tolerate what they couldn't.

But every now and then there was a natural musician who didn't have to figure out anything. He could just always play. And in jazz, being able to play also means having something personal that you are *compelled* to share. This is very difficult when you're a kid. A youngster may have the talent to play music, but will rarely have the confidence to say "This is how I feel! Take it or leave it."

In New Orleans music, Sidney Bechet could do that. Bechet knew he was great from the beginning. At nine he was playing alongside grown men. He had his own band at fourteen. He never learned how to read music. (He could hear something once and know it, so why read?) And he understood the poetry of life. I've heard from older people in France, where he lived and attained iconic stature for the last years of his life, that the women loved him. When I looked at pictures of him, I could never figure out why. He's not particularly alluring. But when I read his autobiography, *Treat It Gentle*, I understood. He was a great storyteller with a mystic understanding of life.

"Some people hear how you've got to smoke reefers, be hopped up before you can play," he wrote.

How you've got to have a woman or a bottle coaxing you on from the side. . . . You can get yourself drunk up to most anything . . . drunk up, or womanned up, or thrilled up with a lot of dope. You can do that. There's many who think you *have* to do that.

But the real reason you play . . . it's just because you've got to play.

"Inspiration, that's another thing," Bechet continued:

The world has to give you that, the way you live in it, what you find in your living. The world gives it to you if you're ready. But it's not just given. . . . It has to be put inside you and you have to be ready to have it put there. All that happens to you makes a feeling out of your life and you play that feeling. But there's more than that. There's the feeling inside the music too. And the final thing, it's the way those two feelings come together. I don't care where that life-feeling comes from in you . . . even if you start playing a number from a love-feeling, it has to become something else before you're through. That love-feeling has to find the music feeling. And then the music can learn how to get along with itself.

That's kind of the bottom line, two profound ideas for a musician. The first is that you have to be *able* to play. That's something you have very little control over. If you have some ability for a thing, no matter how small, it can be developed into something. But if the ability is not there, get ready for frustration. That's why college students and those looking to find their calling are best served by an honest assessment of their own talent.

The second thing Bechet requires is that your life provide you with some kind of inspiration. Now, even identical twins who are raised together don't live the same life. Everybody has his or her own feeling and has to find a way to make that individual feeling fit with the feeling of the music. And many times those two feelings—the musician's own feeling and the feeling of the music—have absolutely nothing to do with each other.

Talking can be like that, too. Using words to communicate what your experience has led you to feel requires a coming-together of your intent (how you feel) and execution (the words you choose). Even when you talk, it's easy to miscommunicate what you are feeling. But for a musician this coming-together also requires a tremendous sacrifice of time and comfort. It takes all kinds of time to develop first-class technical skills, and to expose your true feelings in public can be very discomforting. But exposing your feelings and transforming a bandstand with them is a powerful thing, so powerful you'll sacrifice almost anything to experience it.

Art—creativity of any kind in any field—needs food, and that food is your experience, whether you're on the bandstand or in the audience.

When I was growing up in Kenner there was a crazy lady on our street named Geraldine. She was an old woman, chewing on no teeth with deep, empty-canyon eyes, but she dressed like a little girl and wore her hair in pigtails. Everybody knew she was crazy. You never knew what she would do: lift up her skirt or follow behind people and hit them with switches. As kids, we made fun of her. But my mama used to say: "Don't talk about her like that. She's got a life she's living, too." My mother wanted us to see that she wasn't just Crazy Geraldine; she was a person, with a history and a life that included us.

In music and in life, serious listening forces you to recognize others. Empathetic listeners almost always have more friends than other people, and their counsel is more highly valued. A patient, understanding listener lives in a larger world than a nonlistening know-it-all (no matter how charismatic). Jazz sharpens your hearing because you are following musicians' ideas and trying to hear the human depth of their sound. The humanity in a sound—whether you hear it from your table in a jazz club or play it through your horn—comes from understanding the soft and the hard parts of life.

I remember the difficulties on just my one block. All the women and men were having trouble getting along. One woman killed her husband on Easter. Another man was reputed to have impregnated his daughter. The lady next door, Joyce, had shot her husband, Artemis, for something or other. Everybody was having problems, man. Across the street, my friend's older brother would beat his wife in public. We'd be playing street football; he'd come right out into the street beating her and acting a fool. We would joke about it and say, "William and them are crazy." But it wasn't really funny. Plus his wife was fine and sweet as yams. Thing was, William, when he was right, could also be one of the hippest people you knew. It could be confusing to try to understand all that craziness in the context of everyday life. Because the crazy things stood out and received a lot of attention.

There was a family of brothers who were wild, wild, wild. All of them got killed except for one, Earl, who taught me how to play basketball. But the wildest of them was Jack. He was maybe four years older than I was, but he could whip grown men's asses when he was twelve. He couldn't play street football, basketball, or baseball; his specialty was whipping people's asses.

One day, out of a clear blue sky, he said, "Man, where's your brother that's crazy?"

My younger brother, Mboya, suffers from autism.

I said, "He's not crazy, he's autistic."

Jack said, "Whatever the hell you call it, why you don't ever take him outside?"

This gangsterish roughneck with a mouthful of gold said, "If I was you, I would put him on a bike with me and take him all around and show him everything. Kenner ain't shit, but it's a lot to see if you're inside all the time."

Until then, my conception of Jack had been that he was always involved in some kind of drama that would invariably end in violence. And I grew up with him. I knew him. "Damn," I thought. "What? Nobody in the neighborhood ever asked me about my little brother."

Lessons like that, learned in Kenner, showed me that the surface should never be confused with reality. In other words, you don't know what's in a book until you read it. Life is never all one way. Because in the midst of all that chaos on our street was an abundance of other stories—people trying to take care of their families, people trying to work, people falling in love, people getting their hearts broken. All that on one random street between the second set of railroad tracks and the Mississippi River in a town thirty-five minutes away from New Orleans between 1966 and 1973.

Life there taught you to look at the world and try to put all that happened to you and around you in context—the ironic way of things, the absurdity of it all, the position of black folks in the social order, the nuance and richness of everything. Right and wrong didn't suffice.

That's true of jazz, too. It tells you about the totality of things—it's not about right and wrong. Like the blues at its heart, jazz is about what *is*.

That's why the first question I ask myself when assessing a younger person's playing is "Do they have a broader understanding of life?" (This kind of understanding helps in listening, too.) And then, "Do they have the ability to express that understanding with the sound of their instrument?" A sound is a conduit for information. It can communicate wisdom or empathy or ignorance or whatever. For youngsters, developing a sound can be especially difficult because communication requires someone to communicate with—listeners who can identify with what is being said. Jazz sharpens your ability to hear honesty. It's what musicians call a "bullshit meter." You can detect whether something is true.

An attention-grabbing sound like Louis Armstrong's or Charlie Parker's or even Lee Morgan's can seem brash, but because it also encompasses the cold, hard facts of everything from divorce to dread to betrayal to death, that sound is also humble. At its core is that lonely, solitary, "Yeah, life's like this" feeling—the inevitable, fundamental truth about the human condition. As the old folks would say in church after a lot of celebration was followed by a profound, to-the-point summation, "Make it plain, Reverend, make it plain." The insight of a great musician can lift up your soul and expand your consciousness in the same way a great preacher can inspire with spiritual wisdom poetically expressed.

Success in music, as in a lot of fields, depends on your willingness to address deficiencies in your talent. Even Charlie Parker had to practice a lot. Say you have no sense of rhythm. Since playing rhythms is just a matter of coordination, the best way to work on that is to learn how to dance and keep on beating out rhythms whenever you can. Or you might think you just can't hear. A lot of people say, "I'm tone-deaf." But if you listen to them speak, they go up and they go down in a melodious fashion. A person who was actually tone-deaf would speak in a monotone. Another thing that could keep you from being able to play—or listen, for that matter—is that you believe nothing worth expressing has happened to you. Theoretically, that's imaginable, but I don't know if it's possible. Everybody has some kind of personal and important thing to share. At least everyone I've ever known does.

Jazz writers, for complicated reasons of their own and because bad news makes for livelier reading, used to harp constantly on negative things about musicians' lives. The musicians played into it and loved appearing superhumanly tough. Some really were, but most weren't.

The writers did a great job of mystifying black life by creating and reaffirming stereotypes. TV shows like *Jerry Springer* eventually proved that ignorance and crazy behavior were not the sole domain of the black man. By then, though, the damage had been done. Jazz and black folks were defined in terms of pathology, as if the only thing authentic in life is the literal blues: Somebody messed over you. You grew up on the hard streets; you're a drunk or a drug addict or hard as pig iron. It really is important to be hard, especially if you want to exhibit integrity, but there are many other valuable experiences to convey through a horn, like what you know about life beneath the surface of your experience, where human beings are all mostly the same. Or what you know about the music and arts of your people.

A lot of young musicians suffer from almost total ignorance of American music and dance. Some of it can be attributed to bad education, but much of it is apathy. You may have no musical vocabulary. You may never have played with anybody or heard people play, or you may be off in the middle of nowhere, where no one is even thinking about listening, let alone playing. But even there you can find recordings; they're always accessible. Anybody with access to a computer can get them. If you don't have a computer, you probably have a friend or a teacher who has one. No matter where or who you are, if you're hungry enough, you can access knowledge of culture, art, self.

It reminds me of people in search of their ancestry, except this common artistic heritage is in plain sight for us all. We just don't recognize it. Run far enough from yourself and you're liable to end up in a foreign country trying to find *your* identity in a music you have little chance of understanding—fun to do but unlikely to succeed.

America is a melting pot, but swing is our rhythm and the blues is our song. Know who *you* are.

Misconceptions about his true identity has kept many a musician from really playing. He's allowed someone or something to convince him he can't play. And, of course, there are always millions of reasons you can't do something. It could be your lack of education or the color of your skin—white or brown. It could be because of religious beliefs or peer pressure or your parents. Maybe you started playing and somebody laughed at you.

Everybody has to deal with myths and generalizations. You grow up in your family and somebody starts to tell you that you remind him of his uncle Robert. You know, "This boy is just like Uncle Robert. He's always late. He gets bad grades." He lists a whole series of things that Robert did long before you were born. Actually, you are completely different from Robert, but you start to believe it. Or somebody calls you ugly or stupid. Or fat. Or tells you that you have to be great, and no matter what you achieve, he demands more. Maybe somebody didn't like his daddy and now he is angry at you because you remind him of him. What he's saying has nothing to do with you, but you start to live out your life in relation to those things. It takes courage for you to identify yourself: "Wait a second. I don't have nothing to do with no damn Robert."

Then at school, if you're the one who's picked on, you suffer constant disrespect. Or if you're the hero, you're under pressure to stand up even though you might be someone whose nature it is to sit down. So you play a role. Sometimes you play that role so well that you forget the truth of *you*. And it'll go on and on until some tragedy or other extreme circumstance forces you to face who you actually are. Jazz teaches you that it's okay to love *that*. It shows listeners the many ways that someone can be himself and be successful. Just a roll call of pianists with great yet different styles tells you there's something in the music for everyone: Duke Ellington (romantic), Count Basie (spare), Art Tatum (perfect), Fats Waller (fun), Thelonious Monk (otherworldly), Horace Silver (soulful), Bill Evans (introspective), Bill Charlap (crystal-clear), Cyrus Chestnut (joyous). When you find a style of music you can relate to, it's like finding a friend.

When a family suffered a death or painful loss, old people used to say, "I'm gonna go sit with them." That meant no talking, just being there. You can sit with Monk.

Playing reveals the authentic you. If you're impatient, it will show in your playing; you just won't wait. If you're slow, if you don't think quickly, everybody will hear it. If you're shy and it's hard for you to project your personality, you may have great ideas but they won't come out, or you might overplay to compensate. If you're self-centered, you can't play *with* other people—they have to back you up or lay out. Of course, you can survive like that, but it's not fun to play with you—especially if you play the drums.

With jazz, people utilize their deficiencies in creating something that works. Drummer Tony Williams discovered an array of techniques to compensate for a light swing. Saxophonist Joe Henderson developed a personal intensity in his sound to make up for lack of volume. Bassist Charles Mingus worked out ways to feature group improvisation partly because he didn't know how to arrange for multiple horns.

Of course, not every great musician is responding to some problem, but the ones who do can inspire listeners to invent creative ways to overcome what might otherwise be crippling handicaps. The cliché "Necessity is the mother of invention" applies to jazz improvisation and life, because every day we encounter some new set of variables to negotiate. The "necessity" is jazz. It demands that you invent something that will fill the requirements of the moment. And don't let up. There is a moment at the beginning of John Coltrane's "Resolution" when the rhythm section stumbles and the band almost falls apart. Instead of stopping, they regroup and go on to record one of the most swinging tracks in jazz history. Just hearing that teaches you to see things through.

A jazz musician's primary objective is to create his own sound despite the natural tendency to imitate what is known or popular. Lester

Young may have been the first person to be persecuted for not sounding like someone else. When he started out in the late 1920s, everyone playing the tenor saxophone was trying to capture the big, swaggering sound of Coleman Hawkins. Not Lester. He did things his own way, swinging hard but feather-light, and then weathered the criticism that followed. In fact, self-expression became his theme song: "You can't join the throng until you sing your own song."

When Roy Eldridge was coming up at about the same time, everybody wanted to play trumpet like Pops. So Eldridge developed a style incorporating saxophone-like melodic lines, an intense, growly tone, and hot, fiery super-high notes that declared, "This is Roy Eldridge. All the time." Tony Williams told me that when he was developing his own drum style, he learned the signature phrases and devices of other drummers so that he could *avoid* playing them.

Whether you acknowledge it or not, you're always in some kind of real or imagined competition with the best in your field. In jazz, the standard is very high. That's why many would rather forget all about the past: Tatum, Bird, Prez, Pops. "Damn," somebody thinks, "what about me?"

To address technical deficiencies on your instrument, to learn how to hear chords and chord progressions, to instantly respond to other people's decisions, to learn syncopated rhythms, to master a body of melodies, and to be able to improvise in a musical language—these things take a lot of time. And once you manage to speak the language, to be successful you must speak your own version of it. That, right there, is a long journey not only in terms of time, but of insight and effort as well.

Finally, after that long sojourn, you must find the courage and dedication to keep creating your own way of speaking a language that many people don't understand. It tests your intestinal fortitude and your integrity. It's like raising kids. You know it's much easier to let them sit in front of the computer when they're in elementary school, let them go out until all hours with their teenage friends in high school, then see them occasionally and on their own terms in college. But taking the time to introduce them to new things, keeping up a constant, changing dialogue with them as they grow, being a pain in their behind when need be, adjusting your own "I'm doing what's best for you, child" behavior when it's really what *you'd* rather do— those are the dynamics that make raising children fun. The hard and the easy are all part of one long, great experience. A journey with jazz, playing or listening, takes you through many stages, too. The natural communicative power of this music helps you address all kinds of issues with all kinds of people. Even your own kids.

Today there is an additional set of problems for jazz musicians. The hard fact is that in our time, not many people really know or care much about jazz or if a musician can really play. They don't care because most of the nonclassical music they've heard is performed by amateurs or even complete nonmusicians—people who may possess personal charisma but can barely play. Real jazz musicians were already good enough at fourteen or fifteen to do what most top-selling musical acts can do—and by saying that, I'm not criticizing, I'm just describing.

Most of our population has not been educated in listening, and what we hear on a daily basis leans toward music as wallpaper behind some magnetic star singer or talker or unbelievably good-looking person who does very little more than just be "fine." So the relationship between musician and audience is changed. A musician wants a critical audience that feels the meaning and skill in what is being played. A deeply felt phrase, drenched in the blues and evoking some fundamental human truth, met with a "Yeah!" or "Don't be so mean!" or "Play your horn!" is a moment of catharsis for both listener and musician. When listening descends to a level at which the audience recognizes only ditties whose words are memorized or songs that remind them of some nostalgic period in their own lives, the dynamic nature of communication is lost. Jazz musicians create new things, and we want to make up more, influenced by how you are affected by what we have just created. If you don't understand it, we have a hard time: "You can't follow me so I can't follow you following me."

Too many young musicians today think learning to play scales on chords is jazz. They're being taught that knowing the names of things is the same as experiencing them. All the musical meanings and rituals that go all the way back to the Revolutionary War and march right up past the civil rights movement, Vietnam, and the digital revolution have no resonance in today's corrupted world of jazz and arts education, in music criticism, in the blind embrace of "world music," and ultimately on bandstands around the world. And that's a shame because Americans would like their actual music if they were encouraged to hear it. People all over the world have liked it so much that they continue to follow all of our contemporary trends, no matter how insane.

Today's jazz musicians must have a limitless supply of personal integrity because *more* (professionalism, musicianship, sophistication, feeling) will never be demanded of them—always less. Or something that will sell or that will garner obscure grants. Playing more and more obscure languages can be fun personally, but it's a communication killer, a little like coming across long untranslated passages of ancient Greek in a book you're reading. In jazz, the most sophisticated musicians should consider it a challenge to try to communicate with the most inexperienced listener.

You can't be "too hip" for the people. When you lose the desire to communicate with an audience that hasn't been exposed to your music, you begin to step away from the humility required to develop your artistry.

You never know what will affect people, because music is the art of the invisible. We can easily ascertain external things about one another, but most of life is internal. It's not obvious. No one knows how another person experiences living. It's too deeply rooted, and based on too many unique circumstances. Language cannot express these private, ever-changing states of being. Music is much clearer about subconscious and super-conscious matters. Music makes the internal external. What's in you comes out.

It's like two people who are together and you can't understand it: "I don't see what she sees in him." Yeah, you don't. And you won't. Because you can't know what goes on between them, the feeling the two of them create together.

People have tremendous depth. Dizzy Gillespie once told me, "Man, Charlie Parker would play some deep notes—some *deeeep* notes." And I understood what he meant: deep in terms of his knowledge and awareness of the connected nature of human beings with existence. It wasn't just *notes* he was hitting, Dizzy said. "You can't hear it on a record. You had to be standing there. He would hit a note and it would run right through you."

These kinds of notes harmonize with people. They carry a sympathetic vibration that makes you say "Man, I feel like that, too" or "Is it like that? It is." That's what we need to teach kids to strive for in jazz and all other subjects. That's what *we* need to work on.

Those harmonizing notes are rare, but they're worth listening for. I heard Betty Carter hit some of those notes one night. Whew. I've heard the great alto saxophonist Wess "Warmdaddy" Anderson play like that and have people hollering and screaming in clubs all over the world. I've heard Marcus Roberts just hit a note on the piano and "Damn!" Ornette Coleman can do it. I went by his house one night and we played until four in the morning. Some of the notes he was hitting . . . It didn't have anything to do with the notes themselves. It's just something he feels and understands and can make you feel and understand, too.

Jazz musicians can play to change your life—notes that will help you understand and embrace yourself and other people, notes that are free to holler or shout or cry. And it's fun. Kind of like why children are so lovable. They scream and cry and drive you crazy, but they are so free and mostly honest that you love 'em. Playing . . . It can be more fun than sex. I'm serious. If you are playing with people who can really play, you never want to stop. That's why there are so many long, sad solos out here. It's cathartic, a release. It's direct, spontaneous communication, and you are doing it with other people and they are doing it, too. You can say whatever you want to say, and they can, too.

Sometimes everything comes together. Jazz is a train always coming toward you from way in the future. You hear something off in the distance ahead, and that moment is coming closer and closer and you are getting ready. And then that train reaches you and it's time for you to play that thing that you heard way off in the distance. When you start playing it, when you have cats playing with you who know that that approaching time has come, then it's . . . *whoooff*.

You know how if you're talking, you can make your way toward an idea? Well, in music the time is delineated, so you're forced to work your way toward an idea in the context of time. It's like an athletic feat. You're trying to get to the goal and you have to stay inside boundaries with all these obstacles in front of you, and you are jooking and jerking and making spectacular moves to get there before the clock runs out. And the clock is always running out. Time is pressure.

Then, in addition to musical athleticism—playing and making it through rhythms and over harmonic barriers on time and in time—you have the whole spiritual and emotional maturation of this idea, this sound. And when you get to that idea, it is a sublime moment of "Have mercy. This is it!" And you'll just lean into a note or a series of notes a certain way, and there is no feeling like that in the world. And somebody else hears it with you, and he or she has been been developing the idea, too, and then you all hear it and are together in time.

Finally. Then you don't want to play fast, you just want to hold the note, the sound, the idea, and the moment—*whooooooooooooo*—and just swell up into it and cry.

People hear it and they cry, too. And laugh. I've seen 'em do it over and over again, all over the country and all around the world.

It's a quarter after two in the morning and people are lined up around the block. An all-day drizzle has made it one of those nights that manages to stay gray. The third set is late. People are wet and slightly vexed but still patient because they know they are about to get their fix, the particular emotional satisfaction that comes from bathing in the sound of one of their favorite jazz groups.

They're waiting outside their local club, one of many small meccas of the music scattered across the country. Neighborhood regulars mix with students from the nearby university looking for a sophisticated way to impress friends with their hipness. Japanese tourists who were raised with jazz and love it are there, too. Even if they have to struggle to order a drink in English, they know when somebody can play.

The club has been in business for twenty-five years. Its owner is a die-hard fan who, in order to participate in his life's passion, has sacrificed his savings and endured countless problems with his liquor license, complaints by the neighbors about loud music, even louder drummers, and an industrious panhandler who hangs around outside, collecting money from the customers as if he worked for the club.

The door finally opens and people file inside. The interior is well lit, seats about 135 people, and is decorated with pictures of great musicians at various stages of their careers, some long gone, many with long-gone hairstyles. A tape of some far greater music than is likely to be heard this night is playing far too loudly.

Some of the regulars head for the bar in the back to order very tall drinks they'll nurse as long as possible. The rest of the customers pick their way among the crowded tables, trying to find seats near the bandstand. The tables almost touch one another; sitting at them is like sitting at a dinner table with people you don't know—only closer. The Japanese seem to prefer the banquettes along the wall: If the music doesn't start soon and jet lag overcomes them, they want to be able to lean back and be comfortable.

The musicians are anxious to start. They love this club. It provides a steady gig that keeps them from taking a day job. They love the intimacy of the small room. They are friendly and familiar with all of the club's staff and many of the regulars. But they can't start playing just yet. The bass player is missing; he left to make a phone call after the last set and hasn't returned. (It's funny how either the bass player or the drummer is always late; the two men most responsible for keeping time on the bandstand can't seem to *tell* time once they leave it.)

The musicians have been secretly working on some new arrangements because they want to surprise the club staff as much as the patrons. The greatest compliment for a musician is when someone who hears him play all the time says, "Y'all were really swinging tonight! I liked that new one. Where'd that one come from? Y'all trying to get serious, huh?" They would like to believe that the bartender and staff members go out and brag about the way they sound: "Oh, you've got to come down to the club and hear them."

The staff swears the band sounds better when a group of young women from the university inadvertently drops by, not realizing it's a jazz club.

They're right. The cats do play much better.

The bass player strolls in. The musicians step onto the bandstand. The recorded music stops and the lights go down.

With all the other, more accessible forms of entertainment available, why do people come here?

Because once the band begins to play, they know that for the next hour and fifteen minutes, everyone—musicians and waitresses, the initiated and the unsuspecting—will be united in the purest possible expression of community, having made the choice to become "us" instead of "me." Both musicians and audience are charged with the same set of difficult propositions: to listen to a point of view that's not quite your own with the same level of interest with which you speak; to roll with the punches; to give at least as much as you take. This is what swinging demands. This is what makes jazz great—and what makes great jazz elusive.

It's the last big school dance of the year. People have been lining up their dates for weeks. A large tent has been put up on campus to accommodate the overflowing request for tickets from alumni and students. Tonight, the youngsters will get a new kind of education. This will not be the typical student Saturday night: It's too loud to hear, it's too dark to see your date, and you're too drunk for the evening to be memorable (or remembered at all). Tonight, a big band has assembled to play swinging classics as if they'd never been heard before. Grandma and Grandpa are set for a trip down memory lane. Mom and Dad are happy to be going to something that won't embarrass them, and Johnny and Jane have been taking special swing-dancing lessons to participate in a retro craze that has been sweeping campuses around the country. The old folks are too hip to show up wearing zoot suits or ties big enough to ski on. This isn't some exercise in phony nostalgia for them; it's a fresh chance to dance to America's greatest music. That's the first lesson for the youngsters.

Then, as the band swings into medium-tempo numbers, the elegant romantic interplay that is the essence of swing is the province of the more mature folks—and quite foreign to the young, who are more accustomed to the self-absorbed, calisthenic style of club dancing or the booty-to-tinkle-wiggling "Back That Ass Up" form of erotica that has replaced intimacy on the dance floor.

Suddenly, the band plays a tender ballad. As if on cue the younger dancers step to the side and form a circle around Grandma and Grandpa, whose vertical expression of romance is so elegant, soulful, and full of love that it stuns the youngsters. Nowhere else in American life have they seen older people leading younger people in the ways of courtship. The power of jazz has been demonstrated once again: There's something of a classic dimension within the music that invites people of all ages into the emotion of it. Jazz doesn't have a target demographic; it doesn't carry the label "For old folks only." In a country that now may be the most age-segregated on earth, jazz demonstrates that anyone can swing regardless of age; it has a mythic power to remind us of who we once were, who we are now, and who we hope to be in the future.

When stories of the successes of this music in our time remain hidden, we get a greatly diminished vision of modern American life.

On the night of my senior prom, I played a gig in the Blue Room of the Fairmont Hotel in New Orleans with the Lionel Hampton Orchestra. I sat next to Jimmy Maxwell in the trumpet section. When he was a high school senior in 1932, he'd played in Gil Evans's first band in Stockton, California. Later, he'd played lead trumpet for Benny Goodman. After I played that night with him, he gave me a trumpet stand and all kinds of pointers and encouragement and good wishes. I had no idea who he was.

Let me go a little deeper into what I believe to be the sacred connections between generations of Americans through jazz. When I was attending the New Orleans Center for the Creative Arts as a student of jazz and classical music, Milt Hinton, the great bassist, conducted a class at our school. He, as a teenager, had taken violin classes at the Hull House community center on Chicago's north side. Benny Goodman took lessons there at the same time, studying with the first clarinetist of the Chicago Symphony Orchestra, who was known for teaching students of any color, just as my trumpet teacher, George Jansen, was known to be the only trumpet teacher in New Orleans who would teach both black and white students during the fifties and sixties. Now, even though Benny Goodman and I traveled similar paths and both played classical music as well as jazz, when I met him in the early 1980s at a ceremony honoring Morton Gould, race and generational ignorance kept me from understanding who he was and what he had meant to our music. This blindness to what we as Americans share keeps us from embracing one another the way that we should.

It's a beautiful spring day, but the sun is intent on pushing spring into summer. Thousands of people have invaded the picnic grounds with caps, sunglasses, and coolers full of beverages with varying levels of fermented content. Kids are everywhere, running around, kicking balls, creating the high-pitched feeling of insignificant importance that they bring to every outdoor occasion. Fried chicken, ham sandwiches, and short cotton dresses with floral patterns assault the senses. There's a general buzz in the air that has little to do with the lineup of musicians who will be performing. This is billed as a jazz festival, but most of the bands will not be playing jazz. There will be funk bands, salsa bands, and groups with tabla drums playing interminable vamps, but somewhere in there will appear the music the festival was once meant to foster—jazz music.

This festival is maintained by an intricate network of corporate sponsors who may not care about jazz—or any art, for that matter. Their concern is how many people are likely to come and see their company's logo on the big banner above the bandstand. The director of the festival, who does love jazz, is required to keep everybody happy. He has been producing this festival for the last thirty years and can speak with sadness about the decline in public taste and the lack of jazz stars today, and with enthusiasm about the festival's increasing financial success since it moved away from the music he loves.

In this situation it's hard to imagine an audience ignited by the sound of musicians swinging. After all, the radio is an all-day advertisement for backbeats, and television has an exclusive relationship with the grotesque, super-fast-talking modern-day minstrels of rap and girl groups—beautiful, non-singing but stomach-perfect. The "experts" at the jazz magazines have lined up article after article detailing how dead "real" jazz is, and how all that remains is some high-pitched squealing tenor saxophone, a never-ending bass ostinato, and some super-elite improvised imitations of the European avant-garde of the 1920s.

Still, at five o'clock, a band launches into a blues, and ever so slowly the audience is ignited with the power of swing. Everyone goes crazy, cheering and clapping and urging soloists on to higher levels of inspiration. There is no mention of it in the newspapers or on the radio or television the next day. But we saw it. Those who were there will remember it. And it will happen again, I'm sure of that.

August in New Orleans. The mayor has just passed away. He wanted a jazz funeral—not an "old-time jazz funeral, just a plain old funeral." Musicians from fifteen years of age to seventy assemble on an Uptown street to commence playing dirges, slow, slow hymns, and generally mournful pieces. People line the sidewalks. They know the hymns and some of the musicians, and they all knew the mayor.

There's no sense among the musicians that any of this is unusual. It's hot and the music is slow. Every now and then one of them will shout to no one in particular, "They don't do this in New York!" At every reiteration he replaces New York with the name of another city, "They don't do this in San Francisco!"

In the cathedral where the mayor's final Mass is said, a solo trumpeter interprets the traditional hymn "Flee as a Bird to the Mountain." Some people cry. Others are just there to be there. Some people *have* to be there. After Mass, the same musicians gather in the same street and the pavement becomes even hotter with the timeless syncopations and personalized polyphony of singing horns rising above a sea of drums and tubas all bouncing to high heaven.

People fall out in the street, dancing and singing the melody of songs they have heard from birth: "Oh Didn't He Ramble?," "Down by the Riverside," "Over in the Glory Land," Joe Avery's "Second Line." Everybody is sweating; the street itself seems to sweat. It's not difficult for musicians to create enough heat and emotion to inflame an audience in an enclosed space—even in an auditorium. In the open air, however, it's difficult; the sound never comes back at you and the energy created dissipates quickly. But in this New Orleans ritual, because everyone around the band dances, struts, skips, and sings to a common groove he's known all his life, the humid air itself seems to hold all that energy, compress it, and boil it until the fact of being outside makes it more intense.

People from all over the world come to New Orleans to see these parades, and you would think the city would take an interest in supporting them. You would also think that a ritual so central to the lives of these people would receive special attention from academics. Or that there would be schools to teach it or a special competition for kids to judge the best of the local bands. You would think there would be scores of amateur bands connected to corporations or neighborhoods, like the steel drum bands that flourish in Trinidad or the samba schools of Brazil. But because it is jazz, there's only a handful of musicians to keep this music going without any type of educational or government assistance. Even some of the musicians misunderstand the real sophistication of this art and its significance to the identity of the city and the well-being of its citizens.

Still, some things are so strong that all attempts to kill them fail. And that's why on this Saturday afternoon, despite the apathy of the city fathers, the second-rate schools, and the lack of knowledge among many younger musicians, the ritual itself carries the day as it always has. And the ecstasy it evokes continues to nourish life and sweeten the bitterness of death.

Perhaps that is the deepest secret carried by everyone who loves this music. All the kids of jazz musicians who saw their parents struggle through tough years playing this music and still dedicate their lives to it; all the club owners and record collectors and teachers; all the youngsters who for some reason are touched by the honey-lemon sound of a bedroom saxophone or the brash declarations of a clarion trumpet, the big thump of the bass, or the bing-bang-boom of the trap kit; and all the band directors whose students show up at six in the morning for rehearsals or stay out till all hours checking out musicians in the local club—people like these keep this music alive. They always will.

Swing dancing—the highest possible vertical expression of horizontal aspiration.

CHAPTER FIVE

The Great Coming-Together

One time, when we were playing in Kansas City, Missouri, Governor Bob Holden invited us to lunch. It just so happened that lunch coincided with a very important University of Missouri basketball game. To be honest, we wanted to stay in the hotel and watch the game. When we got to the governor's mansion, in Jefferson City, I noticed something in the governor's eyes that told me he, too, would have been watching the game if we hadn't turned up. I very gingerly asked him if he was a basketball fan. He brightened up right away. "Come on, man," he said. "The game is on upstairs."

We saw the game, then came down to eat. We talked, and he told me he came from a small town in which there were no black citizens. As a kid, he had developed some unusual illness that put him in the same hospital room with a black kid his own age who suffered from the same sickness. They got to know and like each other. It sounded like just another "Negroes I know" story to me until the governor looked at me and said, "We all know black and white folks. The question I have for you is why are we always reduced to telling these clichéd stories? Why is mutual recognition and discovery of community never the *national* story?"

A couple of years later, Louisiana State University won the national football championship and Southern University won the championship of the black Southwestern Athletic Conference. Two schools from the same town. Baton Rouge went crazy. A jubilant Wess Anderson called me from right in the middle of the daylong celebration that culminated in both marching bands playing the national anthem together on the steps of the state capitol. "Certainly, you'll see it on the evening news," he said, laughing. We agreed there was no way it would be covered unless a riot broke out. We did not see it on the news. And no one remembers it.

The kind of mutual recognition and discovery of community that the governor called for and that those marching bands blaring side by side on the state capitol steps represented is an essential element of jazz. It's as if the music were engineered to expose the hypocrisy and absurdity of racism in our country.

Each colonial power created different social circumstances for the people it conquered. The French mixed and mingled. The Spanish mixed and murdered. The English mixed and made believe they didn't. Armed with logic, law, and a Christian mandate "in the name of Jesus," they all administered a tough brand of salvation. There were African slaves almost everywhere in the New World, but in the

United States the slave was a shackled counterbalance to the personal freedoms that *defined* America. He was written into the Constitution as three-fifths of a man. His bondage was so lucrative that it became a national enterprise and cast a shadow over the spiritual identity of the country. It still does.

Even a bloody Civil War and an unfinished civil rights movement one hundred years later have not resolved the problems caused by the legacy of owning people in the land of the free and by the segregation that followed emancipation. Slavery compromised our political system, our financial integrity, our morality, and our cultural life. We espoused all this idealism, all this morality, and all these noble core concepts: equal justice for all, "all men are created equal," and so on. I guess *all* sounded better than *some*.

Here comes the problem. Jazz—America's greatest artistic contribution to the world—was created by people who were freed from slavery, people who were the very least of society. Now, that's happened in other cultures, too. Brazil, for example. In *The Masters and the Slaves: A Study in the Development of Brazilian Civilization*, Gilberto Freyre identified the national significance of the samba. Because the samba defined the Brazilian spirit, it should be considered a definitive national music, he asserted, and because it came in part from Africa, to be Brazilian was therefore to be part African.

Freyre wrote this in 1933, at a time when white intellectual circles in the United States just could not bring themselves to accept the Negro in any serious context. Therefore, America's definitive music was not considered central to our common heritage. We have paid a heavy cultural price for that oversight.

Jazz is not race music. All kinds of people play it and listen to it. They always have. But you can't teach the history of jazz without talking in depth about segregation, white bands and black bands, racism, sex, media, and the American way. We still tend to look at things in black and white. Martin Luther King, Jr., is seen as a leader for blacks, even though he led Americans of many kinds and colors. The civil rights movement is perceived as a black movement when it was really a national movement toward a national goal: actualizing the Constitution. So, too, with jazz.

Even though musicians themselves were segregated, the way they learned music was not. Stan Getz was going to be influenced on the tenor saxophone by the style of whosever music he was attracted to. He was ambitious, he had talent, and he wanted to be the best. Since, in his field, the best was black, he was going to check that out. Miles Davis was influenced by Freddie Webster, who was black, *and* Harry James, who was white. Louis Armstrong's style was influenced, of course, by his mentor Joe "King" Oliver but also by the style of cornet virtuosos such as Bohumir Kryl and Herbert L. Clark. That's how music is. You hear something you like, and you want to play it. What somebody sounded like was much more important than what he or she looked like, especially in the years before television. Our strange obsession with race has devoured most of this history. Instead of focusing on the great coming-together that jazz represents, the obsession has always been "Who owns this music?"

That obsession is still alive and well in America, still wasting everybody's time, still undercutting the spirit of jazz.

It began early. Because the knowledge and intelligence and human depth of jazz demonstrated so clearly the absurdity of the treatment of black people, there was immediate intellectual pressure to denigrate it. Every avenue was taken. One path was to ignore it: Jazz was created by black people; black people were worthless, so there was no need to take notice of it. Another was to trivialize it by associating it on-screen with cartoons or sex scenes—jazz was only good as background music for children's programs or "doing the do," a strange combination that became more closely linked in the video era. You could also make sure it was never taught in institutions. Until the civil rights movement you could actually get expelled from some schools, even Afro-American ones, just for playing jazz in a practice room.

Then, there was patronization and condescension. A standard history of music in the twentieth century holds that there are three major influences: Stravinsky, Schoenberg, and "jazz." Not Ellington or Armstrong but an entire idiom likened to two individuals in European music.

Sometimes jazz was confused with minstrelsy or lumped in with commercial dance music; in *The New York Times* today it is still categorized under "Jazz/Pop." Now it's taught in hundreds of institutions, all around the country, but disconnected from the Afro-American story. (The American story is also ignored, for that matter.)

There were less obvious, cruelly humorous assaults on it, too, like calling New Orleans music "Dixieland," which managed to identify it with the Confederacy's battle hymn: "You play about freedom but we'll make it an homage to your enslavement." And there are the direct modern assaults on *what are thought to be* the brown-skinned elements of the music by those who denigrate the blues and hold that *swing*—the rhythm that defines jazz—is archaic, regardless of how it's played. This forwards the notion that we've innovated ourselves into European art music or some poorly played mélange of Latin-Indian-African music.

One of the most insidious attacks on the music came from people who saw themselves as its friends. Jazz arose, the hipsters said, from spontaneous feeling. Anybody can do it, Allen Ginsberg wrote. "Just pick up a horn and blow." If that's the case, of course, jazz has developed at random and has no aesthetic objectives other than freedom.

The modern equivalent of the beatnik philosophy is the contemporary hipster's love of "all" music. The party line goes: "I like everything. What is jazz, anyway? Whether something is jazz or not makes no difference." The music has no meaning for these cognoscenti. And if something doesn't have meaning, you can't teach it. The no-meaning, no-definition philosophy so successfully attacks the central nervous system of education that you don't even need the other approaches to prevent future generations from playing, enjoying, and being nourished by this music.

Homer was famous for just two books, the *Iliad* and the *Odyssey*. Yet the Greeks agreed there was so much in them that for centuries they interpreted and reinterpreted those texts, seeking a clearer understanding of what it was to be Greek—and to be human. Jazz can provide the same panorama of insights for Americans—or it could if Americans were encouraged to understand it. There's very little argument anymore about its central place in our national heritage. Yet, Americans don't seem able to agree on something as basic as a definition of jazz.

We now have such a poor relationship to jazz that the word has become *less* precise than it was when the music was invented. Now, no one knows what it is, really. We've gone from kind of knowing something about it, through years of playing and discussing it, to concluding that it has no real meaning. The result is that we can't teach it, because no one can figure out when you're not playing it. We work hard to make it as mysterious and obscure as possible, as if hiding it will keep us from confronting some important truth about our way of life. There's a secret: jazz.

Rock and roll has a meaning. Hip-hop, salsa, samba, tango—they all conjure up a distant sound. But nowadays, jazz is misconstrued as all of them, or none, or . . . who knows? But if the music is to mean something to Americans, then its various components must reflect aspects of our way of life. Individual sounds are important, but so is the sound of the group. The process of many becoming one on a bandstand is similar to the path taken by a Korean or Nigerian immigrant when becoming an American. They have to want to be. The process of swinging—of constant coordination with things that are changing all the time—is modern life in a free society. But above all else, it is a *choice*.

Another obsession born of racism is the endless search for the answer to an essentially pointless question: Who does this music belong to? To try to answer it, you have to engage in the futility of deciding which color of person plays it best. Well, if Louis Armstrong was the best and he was dark-skinned, then jazz must be the province of the dark-skinned Negro. But who is the next dark-skinned person who plays as well as Louis Armstrong? And are there some light-skinned musicians and some white ones—Bix Beiderbecke, for example— who are better than the next dark-skinned trumpet player in line? Who is the dark-skinned soprano saxophone player who plays better than the light-skinned Creole Sidney Bechet? Nobody. What percentage of black blood do you have to have to qualify? What about Django Reinhardt? He's a gypsy from Belgium.

What makes a person an authentic jazz musician? Does he or she have to be black and descended from slaves? If that's the case, what about all the black jazz musicians who couldn't play as well as white musicians like Jack Teagarden or Buddy Rich? They weren't black enough? If that's the case, are certain fields—like competitive swimming or orchestral music—overwhelmingly dominated by whites because blacks just can't compete? Or is it the cultural conditioning that makes groups of people comfortable with a reductive vision of what they can and cannot do? "For some inbred reasons out of your control, you won't make it, so don't even try." In the NBA, European players fare better than white Americans do. Is it because their skin is less white or because cultural acceptance of black players' innate superiority is not a part of their upbringing?

On the other side of the coin, the Negro was conditioned to accept and expect less for so long, it became a way of life. In the early days, black people were so completely segregated and suppressed that there was never even the opportunity to sense freedom. For jazz musicians, the first chance to feel equal—and even superior—came when white and black musicians began playing together after hours. Social order on the bandstand is determined by ability. Therefore, people like Coleman Hawkins and Rex Stewart were idolized by musicians of all races.

Jazzmen such as Louis Armstrong, Sidney Bechet, and Duke Ellington began to go to Europe, where they were treated like human beings off the bandstand, as well. They experienced a kind of freedom Afro-Americans didn't enjoy at home. They could have relations and relationships with any type of woman and, of course, because they were musicians, all kinds of women found them interesting. When they returned to America they were lionized and walked with a certain swagger. They dressed well and had their own way of speaking. They earned decent money and played what they wanted to play. These men began to understand that, around the world, their music had come to stand for democracy and freedom.

The resilience and fortitude of true American pioneers is in that music. And it's in it for the black and the white musician. But back home, onstage and even in the recording studio, they were still separated. Among black people of consciousness there was always deep resentment that couldn't be wiped away with a smile and a "Yassah." The more conscious they were, the madder it made them. The more education they had, the angrier they became. This continued injustice diminished their enjoyment of life. These people dedicated their skills and energy to undoing the system that so soured their public experiences.

Writers, publicists, and fans proclaimed Benny Goodman the "king of swing." Now, he had a damn good band, but even *he* didn't think that's who he was—not with Duke Ellington and Count Basie also on the road. Goodman went along with it—who wouldn't have?—but it didn't feel right. Now, what if you were a black musician and *you* wanted and deserved to be the king of swing? Then, it irritated you a lot. Duke Ellington lived through Paul Whiteman being heralded as the king of jazz in the twenties and Benny Goodman being called the king of swing in the thirties.

What if you wanted to be in the movies but not as a maid or servant? What if you wanted to sing at the Metropolitan Opera—and you really had the talent? Then it killed you. A lot of the people playing jazz were those kinds of people.

The whole of jazz, black and white, was a refutation of segregation and racism. The white musicians were some of the least prejudiced people in our country. There's a famous story of a 1926 contest at the Roseland Ballroom in Manhattan between New York's own Fletcher Henderson Orchestra and its white counterpart from the Midwest, led by Jean Goldkette. Scores of musicians gathered for the showdown. Most of them bet on Henderson, whose ranks included Coleman Hawkins, Rex Stewart, and Benny Carter. But Goldkette—with Frankie Trumbauer and Bix Beiderbecke—carried the day.

"They creamed us," Rex Stewart remembered. "Those little tight-ass white boys creamed us." But both leaders had listened intently to the other's band, and after the battle Goldkette hired Henderson's top arranger, Don Redman, and Henderson commissioned Goldkette's arranger, Bill Challis. The next time the two bands met they battled to a draw.

Now, that's a beautiful story because it details the triumph of the underdog white musicians, the black musicians admitting they'd been outplayed, and both leaders being more interested in music than race. But what happened time and again when the Negro won? He was denied, or his victory was attributed to his "natural talent."

Jazz exposed the good ol' American tradition of racial injustice.

Musicians would have been stupid not to know it and feel it and be embittered by it. Generations of people had been victimized in the most profound and petty ways, from being hanged from trees to being forced to call a child "Mr." So-and-so. But, even though musicians felt the sting of racism even more acutely because their connection to art made them more insightful, most did not say, "This is some bullshit so let's re-create some more of it." Instead, jazz musicians concluded, "This is some pure D bullshit. Let's not re-create that in any way."

Most of my own anger about racism came from growing up in Kenner during and after the civil rights movement. It left a bad, bad taste in my mouth, and I expressed it. But all of the great jazzmen I knew, from Art Blakey to John Lewis to Walter Davis, Jr., believed people were simply people. I'll never forget how Art Blakey got on me for speaking disrespectfully about alto saxophone player Phil Woods. And he was right. At some point all of that has got to stop. And you don't have to kiss anybody's behind to be a part of stopping it. When you really get to the philosophy of Monk or Charlie Parker, they were not trying to say that the black man was greater than the white man; they were saying, "By being for everyone, our music absolutely refutes the racism that poisons our national life."

Dizzy Gillespie told me, "Bebop was *about* integration." He said that his and Charlie Parker's objective was to *be* integrated. Dizzy told me this around 1980, when I wasn't thinking about integration at all. "We'll get to that time," I thought. "We don't need to be integrated."

I had a problem with integration that went back to childhood. In 1969, when I was eight years old, my mother sent me to an "integrated" Catholic school in Kenner to honor the legacy of Martin Luther King, Jr. There were just two of us, me and my friend Greg Carroll, in a sea of white kids. Now, when you were one of just two kids going into a school full of students—and teachers—who were going to mess with you constantly, you did not want to be integrated. You couldn't come to another conclusion unless you were a masochist. The constant barrage wore on you and created a new kind of fatigue. My father once told me that he didn't encounter many white people growing up, so they didn't have a chance to disrespect him. Of course, the general abuse was so pervasive he shaped his aspirations to it. But he'd grown up in an entirely black world; he couldn't sit in the front of a streetcar until he was twenty-six years old. Before I started going to an integrated school, I hadn't encountered many white people, either; when a white man turned up at your door in Kenner, the kids on the block would want to know what your father had done to get into trouble. And when I did encounter them, it didn't go down well. Nicknames like "Bozo," "Hershey Bar," "Burnt toast"—that was "Good morning," "Hello," and "Welcome."

You were under a lot of pressure all the time. And that pressure was always to surrender who you were or to accept someone else's definition of you—and that definition required you always to be less than he was. Most of the teachers believed that. So did the students and their parents. It wasn't up for debate. So you were nine or ten years old and you'd been raised one way and now you had to fight for your personhood. Always being told dumb stuff like "You're not like other black people"; "Somebody black robbed my cousin"; "Why are you doing your homework? You don't need to know anything to clean my yard."

Whenever you got into a pugilistic situation, kids would stand in a circle, chanting "A fight, a fight, a nigger and a white." You still knew it was infinitely better than what older people had endured. But their having been *really* mistreated didn't make you like your own situation any more. You could only feel what *you* felt. Something about pain is memorable. It skews reality. You could remember all of the white people who called you nigger or drew big lips on your books or gave you monkeys whenever you received gifts at school, but it's harder to recall the big German kid who defended you or the Jewish kid who invited you to his home.

With so-called integration, everything was different, even the little things. Most of the other kids were poor and Italian, so in the cafeteria we would always have Italian-based foods—spaghetti, lasagna, and so on. Italian food was okay, but not all the time. At home, we always ate Creole, French-based foods—gumbo, red beans and rice. And people would constantly tease you about the way you talked. I don't remember exactly what my mama told me when I complained about it, but the gist of it was "Remember, y'all come from someplace. You got something that you deal with, too. So when you go to school you don't have to sacrifice what you are." My daddy said, "Stop complaining. Y'all are eating, right?"

My parents did the best they could to prepare us. I was reading about Frederick Douglass when I was small, then Nat Turner, George Washington Carver, Booker T. Washington, Langston Hughes. My mama liked to talk about Harriet Tubman, and she took us to see the old Cabildo, where slaves were once sold. I still remember realizing the concrete reality of slavery through seeing those chains and shackles. My daddy and the other musicians were always talking about history and politics. I remember one day when I was in the barbershop with my father, someone said, "You can't win an argument with Ellis; he's been around the world! He's a damn musician. They know. They know a whole pile of stuff." That was just generally the vibe.

My grandfather talked a lot about politics, too. So did my great-uncle. I spent a lot of time with him when I was six, seven, eight. His name was Alphonse, but we all called him "Pomp." He lived in an old shotgun house in New Orleans and was a stonecutter for the cemetery. He'd seen a lot and he could talk when he wanted to.

"It's all in how it hits you," he would say. He was born in 1883, so he could remember what was called the Robert Charles "riot" in 1900. When two cops told a young black man named Robert Charles to move along once too often, he shot them, ran into a house, and managed to kill seven policemen and wound twenty more before he was killed himself. "It didn't hit him right that day," my great-uncle said.

My great-uncle was very patriotic, and I couldn't understand that because he was the type of guy who wouldn't tolerate any shit from anyone. But he didn't feel that being American meant being white. This seemed strange to someone raised in the sixties and seventies, when Black Nationalism was the language of the young and hip. Pomp had been in the service and he believed in the United States.

"This is a great country," he'd always say. "It's flawed but it's a great country."

He didn't like Muhammad Ali: "He'll take the country's money but he won't fight for it. He ain't no hero to me." He didn't like the Black Muslims: Don't come to his door with *Muhammad Speaks* or start talking about Marcus Garvey and his Back-to-Africa movement. No, indeed. "When you get there," he'd say, "they gonna sell you right back to the white man." He believed in confronting prejudice. His motto was "Make people cheat you to your face. Don't make it easy for them. Make them face you, because if enough people let it go, it'll stay the way it is."

By the time I got to third or fourth grade I was ahead of most of the kids in school. I'd heard of Reconstruction, knew about *Plessy v. Ferguson* and *Brown v. Board of Education* and Dr. King and Malcolm X. I knew the names. I didn't understand them in context or necessarily have the order right, but I understood that black people were in a struggle, and I had a sense that something was screwed up about society. And it was clear to me that we were the victims of it. So when I was in history class, for instance, and the textbook showed happy slaves, I was always questioning: "Why would slaves be happy?"

I also understood that the only way to get these particular kids to accept you was to imitate them or be so insignificant that they could just walk over you. It was very tough to come from a black school, where you were respected for good grades and having a colorful personality and where you were a part of social circles with girls and boys, and enter an environment where your positive attributes were considered negative and where you were completely outside of all social interactions.

My great-uncle had made me understand that you had to defend your right to be yourself, and that was sometimes costly. So I was determined that if you called me a nigger, I was going to fight you. Sometimes I won, and sometimes I got my ass whipped, but I was determined that I was not going to act dumber than I was or do anything to make people feel that I was less than they were. If anything, I would do the exact opposite.

The curriculum in our integrated school never included anything about black people. It was as if we didn't exist. It wasn't intentional; it's just how things were. If you came in with a paper about a black person, teachers would just smile and patronize you. "What's this one on? Hmmm . . . I don't know about this." I would always do my reports on slavery and stuff like that, anyway. It's what interested me.

Our neighborhood could be rough, too. Black kids had rules you had to get with, too. If you were determined to be yourself, it could be hard. But you could make them respect you if you won a fight or stood up to a bully or could play the dozens or play ball or talk to girls. You could work out some way to win black kids over. With racism, though, you couldn't do much to change that.

Yeah, racism isn't and wasn't a small thing, not something you just get over. Even now, I'm forty-six and I'm still affected by it. Because it was everywhere and had so much impact—on all the old people you knew, on your own family, on the way TV showed you the world, how the teachers treated you, how the kids related to one another. It could be something as basic as noticing that the white people's streets were paved and yours weren't. And it would go on and on, from that level to everything. Like when we played little league football, there were three black teams and eight or nine white teams. The white teams had every advantage: two coaches, water on the sidelines, hash marks on their fields, practice facilities, parents in the stands. We had uniforms from the fifties, no parents in the stands, one coach, no extra kids to play defense—and still the referees would cheat us. I got thrown out of a game once for telling a ref, "We're going to lose. You don't have to cheat us." You didn't blame all white folks, but the whole system made you angry.

That anger can make a fool of you. The first actual modern jazz gig I played was at Tyler's Beer Garden in New Orleans. It was an all-white rhythm section—Mike Pellera, Ricky Sebastian, and Alvin Young. Alvin was the leader. I was fifteen and they looked out for me, helped me develop my ability, and encouraged me to play. But in an early interview I said something about white people being unable to play and hurt their feelings. It was a stupid thing to say. It didn't take them into account. And it wasn't true. A lot of times your anger at what society runs you through blots out your memory of other experiences that counterstate those wrongs. If you have some pride or sense of justice, that anger is hard to overcome. It's profound and it's real.

I remember telling the great bass player Ray Brown about some of my experiences growing up, and he said, "Damn, I thought all of that shit ended in the sixties." I said, "Man, I'm not even telling you the worst stuff."

After I started getting deeper into the music, I realized that anger gives you a certain power. It's fuel. But it's costly fuel. It burns quickly and destroys everything around it, and as you get older, if you don't let it go, it burns *you* up.

After I reached high school my family moved to New Orleans, and Branford and I eventually started attending the New Orleans Center for Creative Arts, a new arts magnet school where my father was the jazz instructor. In the morning I took academic classes at Benjamin Franklin High School. Those were two great public schools.

The New Orleans Center for Creative Arts was an experiment that was just beginning when I was a freshman. The faculty was unbelievable. Every teacher loved the arts and cherished the opportunity to teach young people. Just the conversations they had with one another made you want to learn things. The foundation of my knowledge and love of the arts comes from the education in classical music, jazz, and vocal music that I got there. I still look back on that experience with gratitude.

When we were in Kenner I'd peeped out that the prejudiced white folks we had to deal with had more in common with poor black folks than either side would admit, but only when I got to Franklin did I start to perceive that there were different kinds of white people. You don't know that if you don't live with them. Everybody's just "white."

I'd gone to primary school with mostly poor or lower-middle-class Italian-American kids. They would fight one another. They would fight you. But in high school a lot of the kids were Jewish. I do not remember any black person I knew ever referring to a person as a Jew. Just white. But I began to notice the Jewish kids didn't fight one another. They had much more of an intellectual tradition. That was interesting to me. I never got called a nigger at that school. You didn't have to fight all the time. It was a much more civil environment. I could hear what the other students were saying. And many times they would want to know what I was doing and thinking— truly a novel experience for me at that time. At Benjamin Franklin, kids seemed smarter, and I learned a lot. Some of the kids, girls and boys, would come to Tyler's for the jazz set and want to talk about it in school on Monday. How many high school kids who weren't musicians would go to a jazz gig today? It was a unique situation, although I didn't know it at the time.

In eleventh grade we were getting ready to study *The Adventures of Huckleberry Finn,* and my teacher, Mr. Keith, stood up and said, "Everybody in this class say 'nigger.' " Everybody began to say it, giggling. This did not go down well with me. Now, Mr. Keith was a reformed hippie and he loved me. I was one of his best students from the year before. He said, "I don't want to embarrass my man, but for us to study this book we have got to be able to use the word 'nigger,' because it's central to understanding what Mark Twain is trying to say."

I said to myself, "I don't like this shit."

After class, Mr. Keith took me aside and said, "Man, if you can't handle this, if you don't even want to come to class, it won't affect your grade. But I'm going to teach this book this way because that's what it is. It's not that white people don't call people niggers. They do. I just wanted to let you know, I'm not gonna half-teach this material, and I hope you stay."

It went down hard, but I said, "Okay, I can deal with it."

I've always been glad that I stayed in that class because the book and the way Mr. Keith chose to teach it were revelatory. He *dealt* with it. And I have always felt that that's what our country needs. We need to deal with all the pain and conflict and absurdity of race. Not dealing with it is like not telling somebody he has cancer because he'll be upset. Tell him. Then he can choose with clarity.

That's how I feel about it.

White and black folks can never understand who they are and what kind of country they can make together until they understand that they are inextricably bound to one another. It's like you have the car keys in your hand but you are looking all over for them—man, you will never find those keys. Look in your hand! It's with you, not outside of you. That's black and white folks. Of course, with so many other groups coming into the country, it seems as if everybody has become a "minority." We talk about "minority issues," but black folks are not a separate minority in America; we are central to its identity.

Jazz calls us to engage with our national identity. It gives expression to the beauty of democracy and of personal freedom and of choosing to embrace the humanity of *all* types of people. It really is what American democracy is *supposed* to be.

As I said at the beginning of this chapter, the fact that jazz is our national art created an uncomfortable situation. The definitive art of the culture directly contradicted the national myth of racial separation and its justification of slavery. Well, what are we going to do, erase from national memory the three-hundred-year-old belief that dark-skinned people were less than human and somehow deserving of the degradation that defined their experience as Americans? No. It was much easier to push jazz away—and, with it, all the sophistication, virtuosity, and power of communication it brought.

It was easier to forget that only during the Depression were Americans so troubled they were willing to embrace the profound content of this music, like a politician who discovers both his wife and his religion after he's caught doing something wrong. It was easier to overlook the entire 1930s generation of great white musicians because they were inseparable from jazz. It was easier to accept pop music that exploited teenagers than to embrace any notion of national significance coming from the Negro. It was easier to accept groups like the Rolling Stones, who *imitated* black Americans and came from England—the country we fought for our own independence—than to accept our own people. It was easier to watch swing, the national dance, slip away, to watch as the minstrel show returned through hip-hop, to watch our musical culture devalued and exported around the world as a backdrop for ass-shaking, wealth-celebrating videos. It was so much easier to define musical innovation in terms of technology, record sales, and street-level pathology.

But then, the unexpected happened: Those tawdry videos started showing black men and white women together in romantic situations unimaginable as recently as the seventies. Those minstrel rappers started making millions of dollars selling ghetto dreams to the suburbs. Negro athletes became unbelievably popular national figures. Black men and women became CEOs of major corporations. And on top of that, DNA research showed that all people came from Africa and that in many instances there were bigger differences between individuals *inside* of a race than *outside* of it.

The hypocrisy, the absurdity, the shame of it all: That was the deepest truth in jazz. And for all the smiling and grinning and yassahing that Louis Armstrong did onstage, that truth is in every angry, exultant, burnished, blood-soaked note he played or sang. Early Miles Davis—the same. Dizzy. And you know what? It's in the sound of white musicians, too. They knew some bullshit was destroying the core of our national life. They recognized the lies that worked in their favor, allowing them to make money and be known as the "king" of this and the "number one" of that, while their black counterparts were ignored. That injustice hurt the white musicians, too, because the music they wanted to play made them want to be a part of *one* America. It let them know how beautiful that would feel. If you doubt what I'm saying, just ask Dave Brubeck.

Jimmy McPartland, Pee Wee Russell, Dave Tough, Gene Krupa,

Bud Freeman, Art Hodes, Woody Herman, Gil Evans, Zoot Sims— all serious white musicians—tried to reconcile the reality of this country with what they learned about this country's potential through the music, which was misnamed "race music," "black music," "Afro-American music," and "black classical music" because of the old confusion about physiology and culture. It placed them in cultural limbo. They had to deal with disrespect from some whites and less than genuine acceptance to outright hostility from some blacks, had to live with the nagging charge that they were trying to "steal" music that was as free as air. How was Benny Goodman going to "steal" an arrangement he paid Fletcher Henderson to write? Meanwhile, the great black musicians tried to reconcile what they knew about the possibilities of this country through this music, with the reality of the lies used to maintain and justify racism. On top of that, they had to digest the reality that black America had little or no interest in the art of jazz—or any art at all, for that matter. Damn, it'll give you a headache.

Still, that's what all those musicians want you to understand: how to express the love of a thing (a country, a concept, a person) that's been corrupted into what you hate; love it with such intensity that you love it back to good health. That's what Miles Davis meant when he asked me at nineteen, "How did you figure this shit out?" He wasn't talking about the music. He could hear that I didn't know anything about the music. What I knew about was *this shit*, the tangled web of lies and deceptions—malicious *and* well meaning—that keep you from achieving your potential and realizing your identity as a human being and keep all of us from realizing the true greatness of our nation. But when we get past it, when we finally address it seriously and overcome it, there will be a renaissance the likes of which this country has never imagined. There will be the great coming-together foretold in the works of Duke Ellington and Gil Evans and

Charles Mingus and George Gershwin and so many other insightful musicians whose strivings for a more honest democracy were never-ending. Because jazz, when played by a group, means "Come together. Be together. Stay together"—at least for the duration of the song.

And in music the duration of a tune represents a lifetime.

Formal education of the first order: playing in public with the great John Lewis. Because of the pressure of playing onstage, one concert is worth two months in the practice room.

CHAPTER SIX

Lessons from the Masters

What I love most about Negro spirituals is
how they put Moses and Jesus, Ezekiel and
Abraham, together in time and then say, "I
spoke to them," as if that time were now.

For me, all history is now. For some reason, this notion is not accepted in the fields of
jazz education, performance, or criticism. Instead, we get the oversimplified story of
steadily growing musical "evolution" that
jazz writers like to tell and retell: impoverished infancy in New Orleans around the
turn of the twentieth century; raucous ado-
lescence in Chicago and New York through

the twenties; big-band swing in the thirties; the birth of bebop in the forties; and then a profusion of schools and counterschools, each moving the music further and further from its blues roots.

The best musicians know this music isn't about "schools" at all. Like my father says, "There's only one school, the school of 'Can you play?' " It's about the individual men and women who can honestly answer yes to that question.

Many of the most valuable lessons I've learned about jazz were imparted by way of stories. Colorful storytelling makes for a community feeling around and through the music. Jazz concerns people and what they do. Just saying the name of a particular musician evokes the whole of their person embodied in their sound. Sometimes older musicians will sit around, giving a roll call of people you never heard of, saying where they were from, and then raving about the way they played this tune or that: "Yeah, man, Little Bobby Moore was a mean motor scooter. Ask Dizzy. He'll tell you. Bobby came into a place with his horn, people start hiding theirs."

Sometimes you learn from masters by what they *do*. In the late 1980s, we played a concert opposite Pearl Bailey, and she brought me a gift to show how gracious musicians used to be when they headlined concerts together. She made a point of telling me that's what she was doing, too. Not that I actually buy gifts for people at jazz festivals— but I think, even all these years later, that I should start.

Tony Williams played with Miles Davis's band when he was seventeen or eighteen. He could sing entire albums—everyone's solo. He was a very intense man, self-contained and private. But he had some great observations about music and musicians. He told me he noticed that the musicians with the best time didn't tap their feet when playing. Because when you're tapping your feet every rhythm you play becomes a polyrhythm, a feat of coordination like rubbing your stomach and patting your head.

The master drummer Elvin Jones was one of the most soulful men in the world. I would get to his house around eleven or twelve at night, and his wife, Keiko, would have the lobster and sushi ready and the sake flowing. We went on several tours together. I loved him like a father. Once we were playing so hard my lips started bleeding. I didn't want to tell him that I thought he was playing too loud. Finally, I got up the courage to tell him. He stared at me for a while and then said, "All you had to do was say something. Ain't nobody on earth above being told something."

Rehearsing a jazz piece requires diplomacy. You need the musicians to want to play your music. You have to walk that thin line between criticizing and aggravating. They are, after all, making up a lot of it, especially the drummer. A dispute with the drummer is a serious thing. The composer, bandleader, and consummate musician Benny Carter was one of the most elegant men in jazz. He was refined, clear, and very serious about the music. I once saw him get testy with a drummer who wasn't playing what he wanted. They went back and forth and things became a little wordy. Benny diplomatically ended the mouthiness by saying, "Use your own good taste. Use your own good taste." The arranger and tenor saxophonist Frank Wess, who had been a mainstay of the Count Basie Orchestra, took another approach: He would inquire, "Why are you motherfuckers playing so loud?" and wait for the volume to come down. It did.

Some musicians insult you with humor. In the summer of 1987, Thelonious Monk's great tenor saxophonist Charlie Rouse went on the road with my quartet. He played some of the most swinging, to-the-point stuff you ever heard. He loved when we would play a wild style we called "burnout"—faster and faster, with all kinds of drum rhythms interlocking with the piano while the bass tried to survive and hold the beat down. One night at a club in St. Louis, after I played a long nonstop solo full of fast, nonswinging 232nd notes, all high, crazy, and nonmelodic but fun to play, Charlie Rouse looked at me as I was drenched with sweat, and said, "Well . . . *that* ought to fix 'em."

When I really think about it, even though I was surrounded by records and musicians at an early age, my tastes were like those of any kid of my generation. Then, at some point, I began to understand that these musicians were great because of the quality of their insights and the powerful expression of those ideas. By now, I've met almost all of the great ones still alive and I've had the good fortune to play with many of them. Others I know only through their recordings. Here are some of the larger lessons a baker's dozen of the masters taught me, along with the titles of a handful of CDs worth listening to. Of course, with jazz everyone is free to find his or her own lessons. All you have to do is listen.

LOUIS ARMSTRONG

I'm always asked, "Did you ever meet Armstrong?"

"No," I answer, "and I'm glad I didn't, because he died in 1971 before my appreciation of him developed." I thought he was just some Uncle Tom with a trumpet. I'm glad I didn't have the opportunity to ever think disrespectful thoughts in the presence of such a great man.

With Louis Armstrong, you have the deepest human feeling and the highest level of musical sophistication. He is down-home soul and compassion, but with plenty of fire. He is built like a bull and could knock you down and out if necessary.

Louis Armstrong is a celebration of the freedom to be yourself. He always knew and loved himself. He embraced the things he was most proud of, like his artistry, as well as the things he knew needed work, like his command of the written language. He didn't hide.

Pops grew up in teeth-clenching poverty as a member of the absolute lowest social stratum. He knew the bottom. He understood that poverty is not always the defining element of poor people's identities. He was raised by people who embraced life under extreme circumstances, and their hard-earned optimism was passed on to him, and then to the world, through his horn.

When I was growing up, some of the poorest people I knew—like my great-aunts and -uncles and my grandma—were the most colorful. You had a good time with them. For one thing, with them you ate good: beans and rice, bacon sandwiches, stuffed mirlitons. Pops always spoke about his "eventful" childhood with great relish.

From the age of eight or nine on, whenever he touched anything to do with music, he was the best. And because he was the best, other musicians looked up to him. I think their admiration and respect influenced him much more than being poor did. When you're poor, you feel bad only when you're around kids who are not poor. Armstrong definitely did not have that problem. When you're a kid and other kids look up to you, it affects you deeply. It can happen in anything: if you get good grades, if you are good in sports, or if you are funny. No adult may have ever heard of you, but all the kids are saying "Play something for us" or "Tell that story again" and, ultimately, "He's the best, check him out."

Now, if you are young Louis Armstrong singing in a boys' quartet, every person who hears your music says, "Damn, this guy is something!" Then you get arrested for fooling around with a gun on New Year's Eve and sent to the Colored Waif's Home for Boys. You start playing cornet and quickly become better than all the rest of the kids. They are looking at you and saying, "Little Louis is unbelievable." There were many great cornetists in the New Orleans of his youth, and he listened with the ear of a genius to what all of them played. Not only did he hear what they were playing, he heard what they were *trying* to play. And, eventually, he played both.

His sense of self-worth grows every time he demonstrates his genius in a different environment. He's always the best—and by a lot. He learns music faster than other people do. He can hear harmonies better. He invents more memorable melodies than any other teenager. He's more in tune. Everybody is begging him, "Show me how to do that." He's outplaying grown men all over New Orleans by the time he's seventeen.

Then, he joins King Oliver in Chicago, where it soon dawns on him: "Wait a second now, I'm playing better than everybody in Chicago, too." He goes to New York to join Fletcher Henderson's band, and he sees he's outplaying all of those cats, too. He eventually gets to Europe, and everybody is in awe of his artistry. Everywhere he goes, the same thing. He thinks, "Hey, all these cats can't be wrong."

And everyone who heard him loved him, except for the dicty people who looked down on him because of the way he sang or because he represented impoverished, uneducated people with natural gusto. He didn't care. Why would he? He didn't have to interact with them. He damn sure didn't interact with them when he was growing up. They weren't having more fun than he was having. And they weren't producing anybody like him. So he's probably thinking, "Okay, y'all might have a lot of stuff, but you don't have anybody that can play like me."

Again, by a lot. That "by a lot" is very important. It's one thing if most of your colleagues play more or less as well as you do, but another thing when you get to be twenty-three or twenty-four years old and no one is even remotely as good as you are. The whole world of popular music imitated him. How many men can say that? He could go anywhere in the world and people would be trying to imitate him. And he knew it. By 1929 or 1930, everybody was trying to be like him: the Poles, the French, the English, the Russians—everybody. He heard himself everywhere, and he was bringing joy and happiness to all those people. How does a guy like that feel? Great.

Louis Armstrong never tried to be someone else. His playing is free of artifice. It's pure substance. Einstein is supposed to have said the equation of relativity was so simple it had to be true. Armstrong's axiom is just as fundamental: It's okay to be you.

Louis Armstrong's sound has the power to heal. His playing is wisdom and forgiveness. He has the sound you hear in the voice of the person you go to when something really bad has happened to you. It can be your grandmama, your mama, or someone else. And that person, through her voice or touch, lets you know it's going to be all right. That feeling's in all of Louis Armstrong's music, that warmth and familiarity and the feeling that whatever you say, he will understand it—and he will understand it from your point of view.

Jazz writing has created a false sense of division in our music, a superficial breakdown of innovations into eras and styles that gives the impression that the natural way of respect between older and younger folks is suspended when the younger ones invent a different way of playing. For example, you would think that the John Coltrane Quartet, exemplars of the avant-garde, would have seen themselves as far more advanced than Louis Armstrong. Well, Elvin Jones once told me that when Louis showed up at one of their gigs in a Chicago club, they all felt like children in his presence. McCoy Tyner, reflecting on that same evening, said, "That man was a king and full of great feeling."

Recommended Listening

The Complete Hot Five and Hot Seven Recordings
Live at Town Hall
My Musical Autobiography

ART BLAKEY

Seems like everything about the drummer and bandleader Art Blakey was a contradiction. He was a short man, but he seemed much bigger because he was so powerful. He could tell you the deepest truth and the most creative lies, both in the same sentence. He exhibited absolute integrity and spoke with moral authority on anything to do with jazz. But he also did all kinds of things that defied standards of acceptable behavior.

Blakey was a pioneer. Intelligent, ambitious, and thorough, he went to Ghana to study African drumming. He realized that American jazz drummers were distinguished by their ability to play three or four different rhythms at one time. He would say, "Never let your left hand know what your right hand is doing." He was a Muslim long before other Americans became Muslims and was devoutly religious in his own way, even though that may sound like a strange thing to say about somebody who had all kinds of women, told the truth only if and when it suited him, and had to have his heroin when he needed it. Stuff like cognac, weed, and cocaine were just appetizers for his real drug of choice.

Though he was often high, being around him taught you not to judge people, because you couldn't judge him. He was such an original, you loved him for who he was. He also would make it clear that you never know enough about people to judge them. You only know what appears true to you. Art Blakey was like the old cliché about the tip of the iceberg. What he showed you was a very small portion of what was actually there.

He started out with big bands and knew how to orchestrate the drum parts to give an arrangement dramatic flair. He didn't read music but could make you think he could, because after hearing an arrangement once or twice he knew the whole thing. And he would improve it—an important skill for drummers, who get little written music or instruction. Drummers must be free to make choices or the music will be stiff. An arrangement might call for some hits or accents, but drummers determine which cymbals to use, where to put the big beats of the bass drum, and how to build intensity or bring it down to a whisper. Drummers provide the grooving pulse of Africa that inspires dance and the percussion colorings that add flavor to European concert music.

"Bu"—that's what we called him, short for Abdullah Ibn Buhaina, the Muslim name he adopted—had superhuman endurance. He loved to brag, "Everybody that got high with me died fifteen years ago." He got stronger as the tours went on. Catch him at four in the morning on the last days of an eight-week tour of Europe and you'd really hear something. During my first tour with his band we drove from New York to Houston, played a gig, and drove straight to L.A. and onto a bandstand. He was seventy-something and didn't even blink. We were forty to fifty years younger and tired as hell.

He taught you with his feeling. He had so much power and strength and belief that you would learn the meaning of playing just from being around him. But for all the informality and naturalness of his approach, he was meticulous about rehearsing and concerned above all about the enjoyment of the audience. "Play with dynamics because the people respond to drama in the music. And dynamics create drama. Rehearse this music thoroughly. Why should people pay to hear a sad, sloppy, unprepared performance!"

He was a big fan of *you* figuring things out. This is an important characteristic of great jazz bandleaders. They tell you, "Listen." And if you say, "I don't hear it," they say, "Well, don't play." If you keep not hearing it, they send you home. In rehearsal, Blakey would play with the same intensity he brought to a gig, and when you commented on it he would say, "I only know one way to play."

As an accompanist, he was a master of architecture who knew how to use dynamics in support of a soloist. From a whisper to a roar, his signature effect, the "press roll" went from a tiptoe to a full-out stomp in two seconds. He was not afraid of giving others the spotlight. He was a generous, inspirational leader who got the most out of his musicians by giving them a platform to do their thing.

Once every four or five months, when we would get out of hand or forget he was the leader, he would call us together and cuss us out: "You motherfuckers aren't playing shit. It's an honor to have a job playing this music and you obviously think this is a fucking game. This is the Jazz Messengers! Clifford Brown. Lee Morgan. Freddie Hubbard. And now your sad, nonplaying ass!" We would all look down and get quiet like children. But it was okay, because we knew he loved us and this music.

And then one day, he would say, "It's time to go get your own band and spread the music. If you get stranded out there and you need to make some money or something you can always come back. We are here." He ran his band like a family. Cats would come back.

When we used to play at Mikell's in New York, all the drummers would come: Papa Jo Jones, Philly Joe Jones, Elvin Jones, Louis Bellson, Max Roach, Buddy Rich—it's like they had a club, a drum thing. We would say everybody else died, but the drummers stayed alive. It's not true now, but in the early eighties generations of drummers were still alive and swinging. And they all turned out to see Bu. He expressed his love for the whole jazz tradition in his sound, in his feeling, and in the music we played. He'd have horn players playing shout choruses and people playing riffs—even though it was a small band. I feel like he always wanted to get back to the big band. He loved that music. I regret that I didn't know how to arrange for big bands when I was with him. I wish he was with us now.

It's hard to explain the love you feel for the bandleader who brings you out when you're young and inexperienced. He takes a chance on you and you never forget it. Jazz musicians say, "He brought me out here," and that means a whole, whole lot.

The word I would use to summarize him comes from the title of one of his albums: *Indestructible*. That's how he was. So we were all shocked when he died. I remember his memorial service at the Abyssinian Baptist Church in Harlem. He had all his wives and children there, a lot of wives and kids. The feeling was so good and everybody played and laughed at stories about him. We all loved him because he gave so much of himself to the music and to us. He represented the ultimate feeling of jazz: easy come, easy go. Not judgmental. He was strict with the discipline of his own playing, with how he expected you to play, and with the consistency of the swing. But he never said, "You have to be like I want you to be." He taught the value of integrity and the power of choosing to have it.

Recommended Listening

Moanin'
Free for All
A Night at Birdland, Volumes 1–3

ORNETTE COLEMAN

A few years ago I ran across Ornette Coleman in a music store. We talked for a while and then he told me, "Don't go back." Now, it was interesting he would say that, because he himself starts from way back. He exists outside the linear history of the music, at once ahead of his time and way behind it, before jazz began. He plays the way someone might have played before people figured out how to improvise on harmonies, back when they just played melodies and vocal effects. His music is a great tool for teaching improvisation to younger kids because it's rich in melodic content and it doesn't require you to know harmony.

He originally based his style on Charlie Parker's. You can hear that in his early tunes like "Bird Food." But he was looking to play with the gestural diversity of talking. He also has a characteristic cry. The title of one of his most haunting songs, "Lonely Woman," also evokes his unmistakable sound. He is a supreme melodist, maybe the most melodic musician in jazz history. He intelligently constructed a style that showcased rapidly changing emotional states instead of changing harmonies.

For a time, he stuck to traditional forms, mainly blues and rhythm changes, but he soon abandoned them altogether in favor of pure improvising without bar lines—just a free flow of melody. As a young man, he lived for a while in New Orleans. One of his great drummers, Ed Blackwell, played with my father in the 1950s. Blackwell said Ornette would tell him not to play in four- or eight-bar phrases. Always searching for a more spontaneous and actual interaction, he would say, "Don't finish my phrases, man," because he was not playing in even-numbered groups of bars. He was playing in one.

His style was innovative because the playing of free-flowing melodic ideas discourages the ad nauseam regurgitation of melodic clichés that fit common harmonic patterns. It was restrictive, however, because harmony is one of the four great avenues of musical expression (the other three are rhythm, melody, and texture), and one of the greatest challenges in jazz improvisation is creating new melodies through harmonic progressions. Ornette challenged the significance of that skill. Many of his avant-garde disciples lacked his melodic gifts and familiarity with the blues. They never developed the ability to play harmony and ended up imitating the free improvisation of European concert music. The confusion between jazz improvisation and free improvisation intensified after Ornette's emergence and led some respected writers to actually believe that Europeans were now the real jazz innovators for improvising in their own non-blues-based tradition.

Over the years, Ornette has maintained the same style of playing. Every now and then he creeps over into the European avant-garde. But he still has that heartbreak in his sound, that genius for blue melodies, and that fire and rhythmic danceability over swing rhythms that make him a jazzman at heart.

He teaches the power of empathy. When you're talking to him, you feel that, somehow, he already knows all of what you are saying and can see and respond to its deeper meaning. He listens so well that you wonder, "Damn, how does he know that much of what I'm feeling?" Ornette hears all the nuances and is attentive to every little scrap of information, every gesture. He teaches us to pay attention to underlying details. Somebody raises his eyebrows—that's in his playing. Somebody wants to glance at his watch but doesn't do it because he is conversing with someone he respects. He doesn't want the other person to think he is bored, so he is caught between listening and glancing. Ornette Coleman can play that, too. He can interpret the subtleties of our interactions more completely than any other jazz musician ever has.

He can hear what you're playing, too. I know that from going to his house and playing with him. Many times when you are speaking a musical language, you become frustrated because your colleagues don't understand what you're saying. You leave spaces and there is no appropriate response. You play softly. They play loudly. You play polyrhythms. They barge ahead. You ask after a solo, "What was I playing?" They say, "Huh?" Ornette not only heard what I was playing, he heard what I was *thinking* about playing. His way of improvising often tells us much more than the approach of many musicians who have a more complete knowledge of music. Ornette shows us that genius is not bound to orthodoxy. You can be a genius any kind of way.

Recommended Listening

The Shape of Jazz to Come
Ornette!
Change of the Century

JOHN COLTRANE

'Trane is perseverance. His development demonstrates the unquestionable value of hard work and dogged persistence. But his life also testifies to the double-edged power of obsessiveness to build up and to destroy.

I heard a tape of him when he was eighteen or nineteen years old. Man, he couldn't play at all. I don't think I've ever heard a musician of his magnitude sound so completely unmusical. You can't believe it's him. He had to work very hard to develop everything: his ears, his technique, his sound, his conception. He did that work the only way he knew how—obsessively—and his work ethic took him from sounding like a journeyman to playing in the bands of both Dizzy Gillespie and Miles Davis.

Long before anyone else, Miles could hear the greatness in Coltrane. He heard the spirituality and country-preacher earnestness in 'Trane's sound. Many of Coltrane's detractors in the musical community knew he had problems improvising fluid melodies on more advanced harmonic progressions. Miles understood, because he had also struggled with harmony as a kid playing with Charlie Parker. He taught Coltrane the harmonic approach that Bird had developed from studying Art Tatum. Bird played a lot of substitution chords. These extra chords fill up space and make playing through a song more exciting. It's like adding more obstacles to an already challenging course. The length of the course stays the same, but those extra obstacles make it harder to reach the finish line in style. Once 'Trane knew what to work on, it was only a matter of time. Like the ninety-nine-pound weakling who becomes a muscleman, he became one of the most harmonically sophisticated musicians in the history of jazz.

Coltrane knew that Miles believed in his playing, but 'Trane still couldn't get his drug habit under control. The downside of Charlie Parker's influence was heroin, and 'Trane, like many of Bird's followers, was addicted. He had already lost a job with Dizzy because of dope and then Miles fired him. It was a serious wake-up call. Coltrane realized he had to decide whether he was going to be high or be Coltrane.

Then Thelonious Monk hired him. Now, Monk's music is sanctified, full of spiritual intensity. Just being in Monk's presence took 'Trane to a higher level, and playing Monk's music led Coltrane to a greater appreciation of his own ambitions and talents. During this period he began getting his life together. He experienced a spiritual awakening that led to a study of Eastern religions, Eastern and Middle Eastern music, and, of course, harmony. He became ever more obsessive about developing an original style. His playing skyrocketed: He practiced all day, every day. And he wasn't just passing time with a horn in his hand. I suspect he had always practiced, but now he worked on core concepts and applied them with purpose.

He put together one of jazz music's most definitive groups with Elvin Jones, McCoy Tyner, and Jimmy Garrison. They played with an intensity never heard before or since. The depth and seriousness of their approach illuminated the fundamentals of jazz in a powerful new way. With this "Classic Quartet," 'Trane reiterated the centrality of the blues at all tempi. He rekindled the relationship among jazz, the Negro spiritual, and Afro-American church music with pieces like "Alabama," his intensely personal statement about the murder by bombing of four little girls in a Birmingham church. Coltrane was part of the 1960s Pan-African movement with pieces like "Tunji" and "Africa," yet still retained a relationship with the American popular song and the tradition of jazz through albums with Duke Ellington and the singer Johnny Hartman. Above all, they swang. Deeply.

The fourth movement of the quartet's masterpiece, *A Love Supreme*, is a written prayer entitled "Psalm." 'Trane plays an improvised melody as if he is singing the words over a low piano tremolo most often heard in an Afro-American church service. There's one line, "He breathes through us so gently and yet so completely," that, to me, sums up what Coltrane was all about. He was a preacher, an exhorter. He wants to *convert* you through his horn. But for all his fire, he is never frantic, never rushing; he is always relaxed and certain. Something in his sound touches us with its depth and compassion, its sheer beauty—a loftiness. It's irresistible. He is so earnest you want to cry.

People love Coltrane.

But then the same obsessiveness that characterized his greatness began to undermine it. Obsession can take you to a point of perfection, but it can also take you over the edge. It's like an overexerciser. He can't stop. After a while, the exercising leads to diminishing returns. Coltrane's version of progress led to the disintegration of the quartet.

'Trane aspired to love and embrace everyone, the way a saint might. He didn't like to deny musicians who asked to sit in with the group. Play a gig and there might be fifty horn players on the bandstand ruining Elvin's swing. There was no time limit to a tune; one song could last an hour and fifteen minutes. There was no stopping his practicing, either. He would play his solo. Then, while McCoy was soloing, you could hear Coltrane offstage practicing until it was time for him to get back on the bandstand. There were no concessions to anything in the direction he took, not for the audience, not for himself. Not even for his band. He let the music go wherever it went. He was just going to see it through to wherever.

In doing that, he followed the fashionable misreading of European art by critics and academics that affected many musicians and artists of his era: the belief that abstraction is the *only* progressive direction for a modern art. It's an old thought. In music, it starts with the Big Man theory: Beethoven abstracted Haydn; Wagner abstracted Beethoven; followed in turn by Debussy, Stravinsky, and Schoenberg, until you get to a point abstract enough to be called "modern."

The Coltrane of *Ascension* was a modernist ripping away the shackles of tradition some sixty years after Europeans had freed themselves.

The notion that you must obliterate the fundamentals of an art to have an important and powerful contemporary identity is almost impossible to fight. There are generations of academics dedicated to this misconception, and they're not just going to go away. There are too many students left to ruin. But by the time you abstract the abstraction of an abstraction, you wonder what in the world you are doing. And once you lose sight of *what* you are doing, *why* is unimportant. The stuff that people still call *avant-garde* was worked out in Germany in the early part of the twentieth century. It came to jazz fifty years later, and now—more than fifty years after *that*—it's still less modern than the music King Oliver's band was playing in the 1920s.

To me, very late Coltrane falls into that "What are you doing?" category. In a few years he went from a super-serious country boy to an innovative jazz genius to a prophet for whom music was only a vehicle to express deeper states of consciousness. And the music, of course, had to sound like a tapestry of organized chaos because everyone knew that's what advanced art was in the twentieth century. So he happily developed away from certain fundamentals of jazz, like swinging.

'Trane went out, far out into interstellar space. His discoveries were very personal. His music became pure energy. Many of his disciples got lost in an abstract cosmos of expression and never found their way home. But Coltrane himself is remembered as a master saxophonist, a genius at integrating the music of other cultures, a hyper-harmonically-sophisticated bluesman and an earnest spiritual seeker. He was all of those things and more.

The trajectory of his career raises questions about the direction of Western art in general. A king of the avant-garde, Picasso plunged into abstraction but came to realize that abstraction was just one part of his palette, no more or less sophisticated than any other style. One wonders why that so rarely happens among jazz musicians. It seems like there's always only the style of the moment. That's too bad, because Coltrane could probably have found something original and significant to play in any style, and then could have kept Jimmy, McCoy, and Elvin in the band awhile longer.

Recommended Listening

Giant Steps
John Coltrane and Johnny Hartman
A Love Supreme

MILES DAVIS

Miles Davis has two lessons to teach us; one is artistic and the other is cautionary. The first part of his career, from 1945, when he came to

New York from St. Louis, through the midsixties, was all about art and integrity. The second chapter, from the late sixties until his death in 1991, was all about adulation and commerce.

He didn't have it easy at first. As an underdeveloped teenage musician, he recorded with Charlie Parker. That was good and bad: good because everyone who wanted to hear Bird would also have to hear Miles; bad because he had to play *after* Bird. Charlie Parker was a virtuoso, perhaps the most fluid wind player ever, but the young Miles was not a great musician in terms of pure talent. He didn't have perfect pitch, and on records you can hear him getting lost on chord changes and struggling to get around his horn. But throughout his twenties he kept struggling to create his own unmistakable sound and style. You don't just go from being how he was to how he became overnight. You can hear the constant application of intelligence and hard work.

Like every trumpeter trying to play bebop, he aspired to play fast and fiery like Dizzy. At first it was impossible, but in two or three years, he developed a good Dizzy-derived style. Some people may have been impressed, but not Diz. Dizzy told him to develop his own style based on his own strengths.

Miles had a distinctive tone, rich with emotion, so it made more sense for him to play sustained notes and leave silences between phrases. He began to study Lester Young and Billie Holiday, people who worked with space and nuanced phrases. He delved into the history of jazz to understand how he might affect that history. And he started to sound more and more like himself: poignant, spare, introspective, emotionally intense. He found that he had the ability to touch people's souls with his sound. It's a powerful gift. You can be a great musician and play fast, intricate things. Maybe you'll get critical praise, and musicians will definitely love you. But people? No. You have to touch people to stay out here. And Miles is *still* here. Like a lot of his contemporaries, he got into drugs, following Bird. They threatened to end his career before it really got started. But his gift eventually demanded he give them up—and he did.

His development is a testament to the value of artistic objectives over technical skill. Miles was intellectually curious. He wanted to know what made his music work and loved experimenting with fresh ideas. He always seemed to know what kind of group sound he wanted. In his very early twenties he hooked up with Gil Evans, Gerry Mulligan, John Lewis, and other young arrangers trying to find new avenues of expression. He led a short-lived nonet whose twelve recorded tunes came to be called *Birth of the Cool*.

He would revel in his reputation as an innovator, but he was really a master coordinator of other people's ideas, altered, arranged, and repackaged in ways that made them unmistakably his own. He began to consolidate material, featuring a way of playing on Tin Pan Alley songs built around the original melodies. (Bebop musicians wrote intricate new melodies on Tin Pan Alley harmonies.) His first great quintet, with Red Garland, Paul Chambers, Philly Joe Jones, and John Coltrane, was built on the pianist Ahmad Jamal's conception: New Orleans two-grooves, vamps, and 4/4 swing that was soft and lyrical with lots of silent spaces.

He was always a shrewd recruiter of talent. Because he had struggled so hard to learn how to play, he knew how to listen for what someone was *trying* to play. He understood the combination of intelligence and soul in other musicians, because he had it himself. That's why he could hear John Coltrane's talent when other people couldn't. He understood how to put together a great rhythm section, and his uncluttered but deeply swinging playing gave them the freedom to participate as more than just backup. His superior melodic gifts, logically developed solos, and flair for musical drama gave his work an excitement and depth that every serious musician loved. He made a string of great albums, including three—*Miles Ahead, Porgy and Bess,* and

Sketches of Spain—in which Gil Evans provided the perfect orchestral setting for his distinctive sound.

His most famous album—*Kind of Blue*—is built around modes: basic scales on which he and his men improvised instead of the complex chord progressions that were at the heart of bebop. He was sometimes given credit for being the first to use modes, but Duke Ellington, Charles Mingus, Dizzy Gillespie, Gil Evans, and the arranger George Russell had all experimented with them before he did. Miles's modal foray, however—featuring John Coltrane, Cannonball Adderley, Jimmy Cobb, Paul Chambers, and Bill Evans or Wynton Kelly on piano—was perfection: stripped-down, melodic, swinging, unmistakably Miles Davis.

His public persona was unmistakable, too—well dressed, surrounded by the beautiful people but aloof, untouchable. He was a guy who didn't take shit in a time when black people took a lot of it. He didn't call for separatism, because he played with musicians of all races. But he determined who and when, and it was always for artistic reasons. He worked when he felt like it and only under certain conditions. He had attitude, a paradoxical presence—great tenderness covered in coarse meanness. He turned his back on the audience, and he would tell people to kiss his ass. But he would also turn back around and break your heart with one passionate note. It became a kind of a rebel-without-a-cause thing. The mid- to late fifties was the perfect time for that. He had a raspy voice and an ironic sense of humor. He was the essence of cool.

But beyond the cult of personality, he could really play. In the midsixties he formed a new band with Herbie Hancock, Ron Carter, Tony Williams, and Wayne Shorter, all younger black musicians who loved his music and loved it even more because of his social stance. He meant something in the community. Under his leadership they developed a new way of playing jazz. And he was amenable to it because he knew how to make concepts work. This group made some of the greatest jazz records of the sixties because Miles knew who to get, how to give them the freedom to play, and when to record them in the proper environment.

Miles showed tremendous courage playing with that group. Many jazz musicians of his generation couldn't get out of the bebop era, but here he was, playing with men who were fifteen or twenty years younger and still trying to adapt and play with them. He couldn't really follow Wayne Shorter's compositions like "Orbits" or "Pinocchio." The progressions were too difficult and the harmonies were completely foreign to him, something he hadn't experienced since the early days with Charlie Parker. And even though he brought his soul and profundity and insight to every note, a lack of work ethic began to show in his approach to form. Unlike when he dedicated himself to learning bebop twenty years earlier, he didn't try to master this material. He just let his sound and vibe carry the music and left the form to Herbie, Wayne, Ron, and Tony. This may seem like a small thing: the form of some original song that almost no one but you and the band can identify. But it represented a failure to confront one of the principal aspects of their new style and foreshadowed a sloppiness that would come to dominate his approach.

At this point he still had unimpeachable credentials. He had played with Bird, had consistently made great recordings, was deeply engaged with the art form, and represented personal and musical integrity to a legion of musicians and fans. You can't find recordings of Miles in the early years doing anything beneath his level of talent, intelligence, or taste.

Then he experienced some kind of midlife crisis and one of the worst twists of fate ever, for any artist in any art form. In the late sixties, the youth movement had swept the country. In music there was R&B for blacks and rock and roll for whites, and it seemed as if there was no longer any room for jazz. R&B and rock were performed primarily by youthful amateur musicians with charisma. They overwhelmed professional musicians with their popularity and power to change people's lives using simpler music, words, and a backbeat. Nothing could have been less progressive at this time than a forty-year-old guy in a suit playing chromatic scales on a trumpet with a bass, drum, piano, and saxophone.

Miles, who had been known for setting trends, was now prepared to follow them. He changed his wardrobe and began to play a form of psychedelic rock that was far outside of any music he could understand. A musician can be great only if he is doing the very best he can with material he finds truly challenging. A snobbish jazz musician might *think* he can play pop music because, after all, it's just two chords and a beat. But it's not that easy. The Beatles are doing the very best they can. They sound honest about it because they are. When a more sophisticated musician tries to do the same thing, something sounds fake.

Like most of the older musicians, Miles didn't really understand rock and roll or funk or backbeat music. He figured all he had to do was get a white rock guitar player and a wah-wah pedal and everything would work out. It didn't. He produced an insipid brand of electro-rock that younger people never listened to and connected it to the noise of the avant-garde to give it the illusion of some far-out act. That era is past now, and we can safely say that not one great jazzman from the prerock era ever developed a great pop band like Led Zeppelin, Parliament Funkadelic, Bruce Springsteen and the E Street Band, the Commodores, U2, or any of them.

Now, it's interesting that when Miles sold out, he didn't sell out to black funk music. He wasn't trying to match Stevie Wonder or Marvin Gaye. He sold out to rock. He was after the rock money and the big rock audience.

There is nothing wrong with wanting to have fun on the bandstand, jump around, let it all hang out. But Charlie Parker and his contemporaries set out to counter the minstrel show convention for black musicians. They considered the seriousness of European masters like Béla Bartók and Stravinsky and worked to bring a level of aesthetic seriousness to their own art that bespoke the depth of the Afro-American experience. Miles, once one of the greatest exponents of that position, now came to the conclusion that it wasn't really that serious after all, not if fame was in the balance or there was money to be made.

He had already bought into a vision of himself as someone who was always on the cutting edge, coming up with a constant stream of new music without regard to his own prior achievements. It put him on one of those hamster wheels, going 'round and 'round and getting nowhere. He had to be hip at all costs, and hipness was now defined by youth and the illusion of belonging to an "in" crowd. A younger lady likes Jimi Hendrix? Then he had to play something she liked. What kind of stuff were they wearing? Whatever it was, he wasn't going to be left behind.

In the end, he was able to parlay his reputation as the greatest of black musicians, the greatest of jazz musicians, into a career as a bad rock musician who survived in that idiom only because of the largesse of rock critics and music industry insiders who said, "Well, if the greatest jazz musician sells out to rock, think how great rock must be."

Selling out always, in some way, hurts the sellout. When Miles retired in 1975, it nearly killed him. A guy with his level of intelligence and insistence on integrity understood that he was being patronized like an old caged lion, treated as if he were still on the Serengeti while passersby stare and feed him potato chips. The lion knows where he is, and he knows things have gone badly for him.

Then, in 1981, he came out of retirement. We were all excited.

"Man, what's he going to play?" Well, he came out playing a sad version of black pop music. All those years of thinking, and that's what he came up with. It was absurd to the bitter end, probably even to the guys who played with him. Everybody knew.

But, after all these years, when everything is said and done, he is once again known for great work like *Kind of Blue*. That's the nature of art. You're remembered for the best of what you did. Not for what you didn't do. And if it's great enough, it will remain. And if jazz remains, the greatest of what Miles did will be there, too.

He is worth studying, especially by younger people trying to make up their minds whether to play for the glory, for the money, for the sex, for people to like them—or for the music itself. Study him and you'll discover the value of hard work, curiosity, and emotional depth. Study further and you'll see that someone never knows when, even in a distinguished career, a lack of integrity can affect you. He personifies that ancient dictum: The best, when corrupted, becomes the worst.

Recommended Listening

Chronicle: The Complete Prestige Recordings
Kind of Blue
Miles Ahead
Filles de Kilimanjaro

DUKE ELLINGTON

On the evening of April 29, 1969, Duke Ellington was at the White House, receiving the Medal of Freedom. It was his seventieth birthday. The next night, he was leading his band in a concert at the Civic

Center in Oklahoma City, back on the road he'd been traveling for almost half a century.

That's who he was, a man for all people and the most unwavering example in jazz of pure dedication and ceaseless productivity.

Duke was the most prolific of all American musicians, and his music is full of lessons. The central fact of his life and source of endless inspiration was his fascination with and love of all kinds of people. It's ironic, because his elegant way of dressing and "always onstage" personality kept people from getting too close to him. But his autobiography, *Music Is My Mistress*, reads like a party. It details his world through a kaleidoscope of people he knew and loved.

He was fascinated by intense interactions and unusual human foibles. Two guys in the band didn't like each other? Make them sit right next to each other. Give them back-to-back solos. See what happens. He loved musicians. Not just their playing. Them. You have to love musicians to want to play with as many different ones as he played with over the years, and to continue to play with the same ones, decade after decade.

More than any other jazz musician, he addressed the rich internal life of men and women in love. One touch of his hand on the piano and the moon entered the room. He loved ladies and they loved him.

He also loved the unpredictability of life; he embraced chaos and found ways to give it musical context. His band was unruly and unmanageable, impossible for anyone but him to lead. Tenor saxophonist Paul Gonsalves sleeping through most of a concert on the bandstand then waking up to play thirty choruses of smoking blues; Johnny Hodges playing a sultry ballad, then rubbing his thumb and fingers together to signal he wanted a raise; Ray Nance so high he could hardly find his mouthpiece, let alone any notes: It would have driven anyone else crazy. Not Duke. Most people use form to defend themselves against chaos; he used form to encompass it.

He played mainly sweet society dance music until the age of

twenty-four, when he heard Sidney Bechet and first understood the power of New Orleans music. At that time, most people still saw the new "hot" jazz as nothing more than a novelty, an enemy of the old sweet music. Duke understood that jazz could be hot *and* sweet. He never discarded the sweet music he'd already begun to master, but he accepted the daunting task of learning a new expression and began right away to mix in the artistic principles of New Orleans music. He would continue to refine and illuminate those fundamentals until the end of his life.

He called jazz "musical freedom of speech" and would tell his men to "personalize" their parts. Paul Gonsalves auditioned for Duke by playing the great solos of Ben Webster. He got the job, but when he got out on the road and was still playing like Ben, Duke took him aside. "Ben Webster *was* in the band. I hired Paul Gonsalves."

His music never got old because he never stopped developing. And while many American composers slavishly imitated European music, believing that was the future, Duke continued to do his thing, inventing new ways to express modern life in the international language of jazz. He was about dancing, vernacular music, men and women, people coming together, and he used that palette to create masterpieces for film, ballet, television, theater, the church, and the concert stage. His career says, "We have our own music. I don't need to study Stravinsky or Scriabin or Schoenberg for greater sophistication. I need to figure out how to do more of what I am doing." And that's what he did.

Recommended Listening

The Blanton-Webster Band
The Carnegie Hall Concerts
Ellington Indigos
The Far East Suite

DIZZY GILLESPIE

I first met Dizzy when I was about fifteen years old at a club called Rosie's on Tchoupitoulas Street in New Orleans. My dad said, "This is my son. He plays trumpet."

Dizzy was standing near the dressing room doorway. He handed me his horn and said, "Play me something, man." He had a real small mouthpiece. I wasn't used to playing that—*poooot*. He didn't know what to say with my daddy standing there, so he said, "Yeaaah"— really drawn out, as if the length of it could help ease the awkwardness of the moment. And then he leaned down close to me and said, "Practice, motherfucker."

Some people think he was a warm and fuzzy person, "Uncle Dizzy." He wasn't like that. His playing showcases the importance of intelligence. His intelligence was greater than his musical ability. Of the great musicians, he probably had the least blues-down-home feeling. I've heard Dizzy say that himself. He didn't have a huge sound and he wasn't the most melodic player, either. That's why his playing didn't engender a certain warmth with people, even though they absolutely loved Dizzy the person. But his rhythmic sophistication was unequaled. He was a master of harmony—and fascinated with studying it. He took in all the music of his youth—from Roy Eldridge to Duke Ellington—and developed a unique style built on complex rhythm and harmony balanced by wit. Dizzy was so quick-minded, he could create an endless flow of ideas at unusually fast tempi. Nobody had ever even considered playing a trumpet that way, let alone had actually tried.

All the musicians respected him because, in addition to outplaying everyone, he knew so much and was so generous with that knowledge. He taught everybody the language of bebop: the drummers, the bass players, even pianists. He thoroughly supported younger musicians in their quest for an identifiable sound and always stressed the importance of learning the piano to study harmony. Diz told me that when he played in the Metronome All-Stars trumpet section with Fats Navarro and Miles Davis, they played so much like him you couldn't tell who was who. He said he liked it when I jumped octaves and played in two registers at once because no one else was doing that.

He was rightfully called a revolutionary, but I think he was much more than that. To me, he was a modern musical genius who understood the value of bringing the best elements of the earlier, pre–World War II music to the new styles. Dizzy wanted to keep it all: dancing, comedy, a relationship with the theater through floor shows, the kinship with Latin music.

He wanted to play across generations, too. He made records with Roy Eldridge and Duke Ellington from the previous generation, to mention just two of many, and he brought a lot of young musicians into the music, including John Lewis, Lalo Schifrin, Melba Liston, John Coltrane, Danilo Perez, and Giovanni Hidalgo.

He had ambitions for jazz. He helped develop the Cubop style to restore the link between jazz and the music of Cuba that Jelly Roll Morton had called "the Spanish tinge." He didn't completely understand the technical part of Latin music, but understood the importance of playing it as a way to bring people together. That's why his last big band was called the United Nations Orchestra and included great musicians from Panama, Brazil, Puerto Rico, and Argentina. Everybody who played with him loved him.

He embraced the big-band tradition, too. "Don't let that big band go," he told me once after a concert at Jazz at Lincoln Center. "To lose our orchestral music should not be considered an achievement." Charlie Parker might have had a deeper talent for music than Dizzy did, but Dizzy had a deeper sense of the music's place in our culture.

I gave a real wild interview once when I was twenty. I said all sorts of things in an indelicate manner about people selling out and ignorant jazz writers and how nobody was shit except—by implication—me. A lot of people got mad.

A few weeks later, I saw Dizzy backstage at the Saratoga Jazz Festival. He beckoned to me, then opened up his trumpet case. He had that interview in there.

I said I was trying to live it down.

He said, "No, noooo. Say what you believe to be true. But you can't talk like that and escape unscathed. Be ready for the return, be ready for the return. It might not *ever* stop. You don't really understand the price of words yet, but you're about to be given a good understanding."

I told you Dizzy was very intelligent.

Recommended Listening

Dizzy Gillespie and His Sextets and Orchestra: Shaw 'Nuff!
Dizzy Gillespie, Sonny Rollins, and Sonny Stitt: Sonny Side Up
Dizzy on the French Riviera

BILLIE HOLIDAY

I once listened to almost nothing but Billie Holiday for an entire year. I was about twenty-four, maybe a little older. I listened to her records and music nonstop, trying to figure out where she was coming from. Very interesting things become clear when you listen to her.

She had a limited range. She wasn't virtuosic. She didn't scat-sing. She didn't ever solo, exactly. Her solo was what she did with the melody and what she brought to the rephrasing of a song. She was influenced by Louis Armstrong and could give you the feeling that you were floating across time itself. She imbued ballads and torch songs with a much deeper meaning, and with unerring rhythm she swung like crazy at every tempo. Sad song / happy dance: that all-important paradox in her sound enriched her music-making.

Everybody knows her pathology. She was raped, was a prostitute, drank and got high and suffered all kinds of bad treatment, got busted, had her cabaret card confiscated and couldn't work. She took prejudice *hard*. Everybody isn't resilient about that kind of stuff. But that's not what's most important about her. Many people live the colorful, downtrodden life. None of them sing like Billie Holiday. Yes, there is tragedy in her sound but its core is affirmative.

I love *Lady in Satin*, the last record she made. My father used to play it when I was growing up. Some people hate it because so little of her voice is left. But for me, it teaches that the message you are delivering can be more important than limitations in the method of delivery. Billie could evoke dark, dark feelings by applying swinging sweetness. If you put a little salt in something sweet, it gets sweeter; if you put some sugar in something bitter, it gets more bitter. She was like that.

Recommended Listening

Lady Day: The Complete Billie Holiday on Columbia (1933–1944)
The Complete Billie Holiday on Verve, 1945–1959
Lady in Satin

JOHN LEWIS

Sometimes musicians will create a kind of street persona to go with jazz. It comes from the "We was born in the street, we grew up with a barrel of butcher knives" tradition of Louis Armstrong and Jelly

Roll Morton. Miles Davis did that; he was the son of a dentist and gentleman farmer but didn't want anybody to know it. Think about it. How many people can really grow up like Louis Armstrong? You're going to have a very small talent pool if everyone has to go through that.

There was a tendency among some writers and musicians to discredit John Lewis because he loved European music and talked about it, because his music was so clear and to the point, because he didn't get drunk or high, didn't have a loud mouth, wasn't a study in pathology. But the unbelievably high quality of the music he left us wipes all that out. The last two CDs he made—*Evolution I* and *Evolution II*—are like great poems.

I remember one time I asked my father if my sound was too clear to be a jazz sound.

He said, "Man, what's a jazz sound?"

"You know, like Pops."

"Pops's sound wasn't clear? There's no such thing as a jazz sound. There's just a *sound*."

John Lewis understood that. He cut across so many clichés about jazz music and jazz musicians. He got right to the heart of the matter. He was about music; that was all. The first time I played a concert with him, I was tired at the end of an hour and a half. Really tired. Now, I was used to playing with all kinds of young musicians who played loud and long. With them, you are prepared for a real physical way of playing. But John Lewis exhausted me with his intensity. We rehearsed a lot, but I didn't understand the level of seriousness he was going to bring to the gig. When I say seriousness, I mean the intention to focus on every moment of the music—listening, playing, nothing extraneous or without meaning. Absolutely nothing. I mean not one single note for ninety straight minutes. I was sitting in the well of the piano, and when you sit in the center of that much intensity the energy of it wears you down. It's like being in the sun for a long time. You may not be aware of it, but after an hour and a half of it you look up and you're soaking wet. John was that sun.

We once did a gig in honor of Dizzy out in New Jersey, the kind of thing that had a lot of trumpet players, a lot of bass players, and it seemed like 250 musicians. We all got up on the stage to play "'Round Midnight." I knew everybody would play loud. The sound was not mixed right. It was a recipe for disaster, and I remember looking at John and thinking before we started, "I wonder what he's going to do now because the environment is not controlled." I thought of him with the Modern Jazz Quartet that he led for forty years. There, everything was in balance, everybody at the right volume. Anyway, I played a sad solo, trying to be heard above all this noise. Then John played. He played exactly the way he always did and everybody on-stage immediately brought the volume down so he could be heard. He got the loudest and most sustained ovation of the night.

How did he do it? It's hard to explain, but his approach teaches the power of insistence—insistence on value and quality ideas. When I played extraneous ideas, he would shake his head and say, "Make sure you play a melody before doing all kinds of elaborate variations." He once conducted the Jazz at Lincoln Center Orchestra in a concert of Duke Ellington's music. I wasn't playing and had never heard the band play with such control and balance. I asked Wess Anderson, "What did he do to get y'all to play in balance and swing so hard?"

Wess replied, "He just stood there and looked at us, and we knew we were bullshitting. He kept looking and waiting for us to play it right and we did." Now, that's the telekinetic power of a master.

On every gig, he played these compact themes that were rich with information, and he would insist on our dealing with them. Whatever happened, he wouldn't change that. He made you go with him and therefore with the music. It's like when someone talks to you always at the same volume and looks right at you the whole time and the intensity of the way he or she looks at you makes the bullshit in your thinking immediately evident. You start feeling insecure. You don't have to say a word. Purify your thinking and your participation or leave. That's what playing with him was like. Play or get off the bandstand.

He might tell you a thing or two: "Listen to this record—it will help your vocabulary. Learn from the vocabulary." Developing an improvised solo was like catching fish, he used to say. "You pull some into the boat and you throw some back. But every now and then you will find a good one, and when you find a good one, keep him because now you have something to make a meal. If you fix him right he can go a long way."

John Lewis didn't fall into a category. He could play in the style of Duke or Louis Armstrong or Teddy Wilson and still be pure John. But he also belonged to the first generation of beboppers. He played in the Dizzy Gillespie big band, he wrote great arrangements, and he led the Modern Jazz Quartet. He knew a lot about the arts. He was erudite. He understood the blues above all else. Now, the way he presented himself didn't make you think about the blues. He wasn't clichéd, not some guy from Mississippi with a guitar who's going to be poisoned because he took somebody's woman. But, boy, he knew about the blues. At every moment, wherever he was, he was going to find the blues.

John would insist on the truth. He would talk to you directly and honestly. It was exactly the way he played. When he told you something he thought you wouldn't like, he would wait to hear what you had to say. And he would respond to it. He could be very complimentary, too, and a compliment from him meant a lot, because you knew it was honest.

He loved his wife, Mirjana. A concert wasn't finished until she gave him her assessment. I used to love to go over to their apartment just to be in their aura, because of the feeling the two of them had. He relied on her. She's a musician, too, with great taste, and she loved him deeply and would make intelligent, insightful comments. It was interesting to see them together. They didn't ever engage in trivial badgering of each other. They loved music and they loved art and they loved each other and they were about that.

I used to play with him in his living room. He would sit down, spread his music out, very organized, like it was a concerto or something, and then he would start to play all kinds of stuff that didn't have anything to do with the sheet music. His sound was so pure and good, each note would be like a pearl. I would laugh sometimes at the way he looked at the music as if he were actually playing it. Then he'd start humming along with himself. I asked him one time if that was on the music, too. He said, "You missed your entrance." And kept swinging.

Recommended Listening

MJQ: 40 Years
Evolution
Evolution II

THELONIOUS MONK

Monk is an interesting study in contradictions because his behavior was eccentric—wearing strange hats, dancing 'round and 'round while others soloed, employing long periods of silence—but his music is not eccentric at all. It's very logical, mathematical, and coherent. His improvisations show more attention to consistent thematic development than any other jazz musician's. He gets an idea and then plays it up and down and forward and backward. He liked to say that musicians were mathematicians.

Monk had the sound of the church in his playing, and he had the spiritual inevitability that comes only to somebody who knows the depth of the human soul. It made him at once wise and childlike, a rare combination in a full-grown man. Children don't usually sort through things to remove the painful truth. Monk gave you that kind of cut-to-the-bone honesty with the oversight of a genius. He had a ring with MONK on it and would turn it upside down so that it read KNOW. One of his albums is called *Always Know.*

He was a great titler of tunes, probably the greatest in the music: "Coming on the Hudson," "Trinkle Tinkle," "Green Chimneys," "Crepuscule with Nellie." If there was an award for putting names to tunes, he'd get it.

Monk didn't run up and down the keyboard in flurries like James P. Johnson, Willie "The Lion" Smith, "Fats" Waller, or the other sophisticated East Coast pianists he admired most. He had another kind of virtuosity: getting notes to bend and creak and moan. His style was neither old-fashioned nor modern. He played in a swing-era, 1930s shuffle time, but he was also the chief architect and high priest of 1940s bebop, a style that is still recognized as the dividing line between modern and premodern jazz. He came up with his own way of addressing the fundamentals of the music (*Monk Plays Duke Ellington*), his own way of playing fast material (*Four in One*), his own way of negotiating melodies through harmonic progressions (*In Walked Bud*), and his own way of playing the blues (*Blue Monk*). All of it is distinctive and was met with great criticism, even among some musicians. They said Monk couldn't play or that other musicians played his tunes better than he did. Most critics hated him. Then he lost his cabaret card taking a fall for Bud Powell in a drug bust. Through it all, Monk kept doing things his own way, and because he succeeded at being himself, he gives you the confidence that you can do that, too.

He had a quirky personality. His son gave me a money clip Monk carried. He told me that Thelonious would keep a thousand-dollar bill in it and when anybody asked him for money, he would pull it out and say, "Can you change this thousand?" That's how he looked at things—from the opposite side.

Somebody would ask him, "What's happening, Monk?"

"Everything is happening all the time, man."

Recommended Listening

Solo Monk
The Complete Riverside Recordings
Live at the It Club

JELLY ROLL MORTON

Jelly Roll teaches us the joy of engagement. He found inspiration in the rich culture of turn-of-the-century New Orleans. He loved the preachers, the prostitutes, and the parlor pianists. It's ironic that he would become the music's first great composer, intellectual, and raconteur, because his upbringing had nothing to do with "night people" and "good times." He was a New Orleans Creole, and many Creoles were highfalutin, especially in those days. To them, the highest form of music was light opera performed on the piano. Not Bach or Chopin or even Gottschalk, but the lightest version of classical music. Whatever had all the trappings of European sophistication without the substance—that's what they loved. And they took a dim view of Negroes. "A Negro is dumber than two dead police dogs in somebody's backyard," Jelly told the trumpeter Jacques Butler when Butler referred to them both as Negroes.

But in the recordings he made for the Library of Congress with Alan Lomax—in the music he plays and what he says—it's crystal clear that Jelly Roll had an intimate knowledge of the full range of people he had encountered during his lifetime, and while he may have been prejudiced toward some people, he was not prejudiced toward anybody's music.

As a boy, he was attracted to the wildest side of New Orleans nightlife, where people of all colors and all classes met and merged. Jelly Roll observed that when you go low enough, everyone is equalized by his or her common pursuits. He and Sidney Bechet became the two great traveling missionaries for New Orleans music. But Morton was the first to write down New Orleans polyphony—the clarinet, trumpet, and trombone lines, all playing different melodies at once. He and Duke Ellington are the only two who ever really wrote that counterpoint well. He codified the chorus format, too, which allowed him to fit one section of a piece seamlessly into other sections. This diversity of form led everyone away from endless repetition of the same harmonies. (Check out "Black Bottom Stomp" or "The Pearls.")

In the Library of Congress recordings, he explained all kinds of things about syncopation, balance, riffs, breaks, and call and response. He also understood that certain musical devices were uniquely American and significant. And that those things were specifically representative of our way of life. For his time, for where he came from, his experiences and explanations must have seemed like ancient Greek to the people around him.

Even more profound than his knowledge of the music was his understanding of its meaning. It's possible for a person with a good memory to learn a lot of music, but Jelly Roll Morton knew the music was important, knew where it fit on history's time line and understood the artistic achievements of his contemporaries. New Orleans didn't produce anyone else even remotely like him.

He engendered a lot of bad feelings because he loved to talk about what he had done and what was wrong with what everyone else was doing. I think Jelly Roll could never get over the injustices of his time. He was hurt by racism, by the music publishing industry that failed to pay him what he was worth, and eventually by the fact that musical tastes changed. He was considered an old-timer, eclipsed by Duke Ellington and others, when he wasn't even that old. In a time when you were sure to get ripped off, he was always vocal about it. It was kind of like being a loud slave—it didn't make for long-term happiness.

Jelly was a rich source of the kind of information that reveals jazz music as part of a *world:* "The community did *this,* and in response we played *that.*" Jazz needs his vision today because the music is now taught as something removed from everyday experience, some elite specialty for outsiders. When listening to Jelly Roll you can hear his whole world: There are street sounds in it, parades, death, church music, humor, fighting, Caribbean dances, Italian songs, whorehouse accompaniments, levee tunes, Indian chants, ragtime, stomps, slow drags, and romantic ballads—every kind of music and activity.

For all of Jelly's arrogance and self-importance, the richness of his music tells us that he was engaged with many different kinds of people—from the refined and high-and-mighty to the coarse and low-down. He plays their lives as if he were inside of them, and when his music is heard they come alive again.

Recommended Listening

The Complete Library of Congress Recordings
1923–1924
1926–1930

CHARLIE PARKER

Above all, Bird demonstrates the limitless potential of the mind to think fast and logically over long periods of time. Before Bird, super-virtuosic fast passages were reserved for insubstantial but tricky effects, such as the variations on "The Carnival of Venice," or other kinds of transitional material that led to more memorable themes. But with Charlie Parker the fast playing *is* the theme. The ability to invent compelling, meaningful melodies at breakneck speed is his most astonishing musical achievement. A lot of people have tried to imitate him. No one has ever come close.

It took time for him to develop this way of playing; his triumphs were hard-won. But when musicians heard his developed style on record, they all tried to improvise in his style regardless of their instrument. It's hard to describe the brilliance of Bird's playing. You have to experience it for yourself: the supreme logic, the perfect time, the purity, and the poetry and soul of it all, no matter the pace. And, for all its complexity, it seemed to speak to everybody. John Lewis told me all kinds of people would be at Charlie Parker's gigs. It always shocked him: sailors, firemen, policemen, city officials, prostitutes, dope fiends, just regular working people—whoever it was, when Bird started playing, his sound would arrest the room. Everybody would sit or stand there and listen with their mouths open. The music had so much in it because it had come such a long distance. It had all of American music in it: fiddler's reels and Negro spirituals; camp-meeting shouts; minstrel ditties, vaudeville tunes, and American popular songs; the blues and ragtime; parlor music; European classical music—and the irresistible stomping, riffing style of blues playing that tells you Parker came from Kansas City.

But there's another lesson Bird teaches us: the necessity for supremely gifted people to put their talent first. Because in the end, dope, not art, consumed Bird's life and limited the development of his music. We are still compelled to study him because he was a true genius. But it's ironic that this most balanced of musicians—who could play with blinding speed and never lose his equilibrium, create all these perfect melodies through the most sophisticated harmonies, sit in with bands and play phenomenal solos on songs he didn't even know, and have such a natural feeling for so many different kinds of people—could be so unbalanced in his life outside of music.

His story would have been much more triumphant if not for dope. That's not said in the way of judgment. As my great-uncle used to say, "You don't know how life hit him." Sometimes circumstances hit you so hard you actually can't function. Bird had all kinds of insights. He tried to integrate his world, tried to elevate people, tried to establish his art as equal to other arts. And he did those things in the face of a culture that didn't want him. So the kind of insults other people walked past every day—well, maybe Bird's heart and soul just couldn't handle them.

Recommended Listening

The Complete Savoy Sessions
Charlie Parker with Strings
One Night in Birdland

MARCUS ROBERTS

Marcus Roberts is a modern genius, a musician of unmistakable originality and soul—and an even more remarkable person. For all who wish to discover the artistry of a master jazz musician in the post-rock era, study Marcus.

I first met him in 1983 at the Jacksonville Jazz Festival. I'd heard about him earlier because he was one of the only blind instrumentalists trying to play jazz at that time. A year or two later I heard him in a master class I conducted at Florida State University. He played

"Stella by Starlight" and sounded pretty good. But there's no way that performance, full of fusion and pop music clichés, gave any indication of who was sitting before us.

In the early eighties, I was interested in any young musician who wanted to play. I gave Marcus my number. He started calling me to ask questions about the music. Even though I loved his seriousness, in those days I wasn't the most respectful person to talk to on the telephone and was always short with him. I kept telling him, "Man, learn this, do that." Or I'd play eight bars of Monk on the piano and pretend I could play the whole thing: "I'm a trumpet player and I know this music. Why don't you?" But he choked down the disrespect and kept calling.

I noticed that he was extremely intelligent. His range of interests and ability to understand the problems of playing jazz in our time stood out. I also noticed he was stubborn and determined to express his point of view. You couldn't push him around. So enduring my attitude was difficult, but he put up with it because he really, truly wanted to play. Nevertheless, he already had his way and he believed in it, and if he didn't agree with you, he was not afraid to tell you so.

He came to New York and sat in with my quintet in 1983 or early '84, but Kenny Kirkland was playing so much piano then, I couldn't hear Marcus at all. When Kenny and Branford left the band in 1985, I didn't really know what to do or who to call. I was hurt because my guys had left me to play rock music. I didn't even know if I wanted to keep playing jazz. I thought about playing only classical music. Jazz was so difficult with no supportive infrastructure. Most of the music writers were celebrating my loss. After all, I had not been content to leave all the thinking to them in the typical "Yassuh, Boss" style of the day. And I was an outspoken critic of the popular music they loved and made a living elevating. Most jazz people could not have cared less.

I was desperate to find people to play with, but there weren't that many my age who even wanted to play. Plus, I still didn't know if it was possible for me to be really good. I had already received a lot of attention, which created some jealousy in those who could play better and had been out there a lot longer. So I also felt guilty. I knew I could get to a higher level, but how could I get beyond that? Who could play with the kind of originality and spark I needed? Who had the belief?

Almost as a last resort I called Marcus, not because of his playing but because of his honesty. When he came out to play it was a revelation. I had never been around a blind person. The first lesson he taught me was that you can't make it by yourself. I didn't have that much faith in other people. I had just lost my band. I always felt that I had to do things on my own. Marcus made it clear that you can't: "None of this music is about you by yourself. It's about you with other people. You've got to come to grips with that."

Vernon Hammond, our road manager, had sent him some tapes of our gigs. Some of them, like *Black Codes* (*From the Underground*), were very complicated. Marcus arrived knowing every tune. So we knew he was serious, but he really struggled on that first tour. We were used to the power of Kenny Kirkland, and Marcus didn't have that big sound yet. The tour lasted about a month and a half. Then we had a two- or three-week break. When Marcus came back after that break it was like another person sitting behind the piano.

That's when we started calling him "The J Master." (When I was growing up, if a musician was playing well you'd say, "He put some Johnson on it." So Marcus was "J'ing," and that led us to the ultimate compliment—the honorable *J Master*.)

Marcus grew up in the church, where he absorbed a natural feeling for the blues and human expression. His blindness qualified him for a special school, which removed him from a rough social environment. He did unbelievably well in high school and college, where he maintained a 3.7 grade point average, even though he had to take notes in Braille at night after taping lectures during the day.

After joining the band, he used that work ethic to systematically learn the history of the piano, Jelly Roll, Duke, Monk, and Bud Powell. Now, he didn't go through the tradition to "find himself." Sometimes you're told you have to go through things to do that. But either you're yourself or you're not. He was always himself. This originality is in his touch on the piano: light yet weighty, elegant but "dirgey," in the words of Wess "Warm Daddy" Anderson, an authority in these matters. Wess and I were talking just the other day about what a shame it is that J's music is not much more widely known, because it's so diverse and thoroughly enjoyable. I'll include references to specific tunes as I discuss his playing so you can check it out for yourself.

He is unparalleled as an accompanist in our time: great riffs, inventive call and response, quick-witted rhythmic sophistication. (Check out "The Arrival" from *The Truth Is Spoken Here*.) He has a completely innovative way of extending material ("The Easy Winners" from *The Joy of Joplin*), his own way of playing the blues ("Nothin' Like It" from *In Honor of Duke*) and American popular songs ("Mona Lisa" from *Cole After Midnight*), and he has his own conception of grooves and exotic melodies ("Nebuchadnezzar" from *Deep in the Shed*). His "Spiritual Awakening," also from *Deep in the Shed*, is one of the deepest melodies written in the last forty years.

A lot of what he knows is on his record *Blues for the New Millennium:* all kinds of forms, orchestration, and color, and the combination of modern rhythmic conceptions sin-dipped in country blues ("A Servant of the People" and "Whales from the Orient" speak eloquently to this fact). He's also one of the few post-bebop piano players who can play with both hands, and he can do it better than anyone in our generation. What he does with time—like his many versions of "Cherokee"—no one else has ever been able to do. He is a master of all aspects of piano playing—accompanying and soloing in a large group, by himself, and as the solo voice in a trio ("Harvest Time" from *Time and Circumstance*).

He could learn my extended pieces, like "Blue Interlude" or "Citi Movement," before the rest of us. I would play the piano part for him while the rest of the band read through theirs. He would immediately learn his music and then start correcting what we were playing. "Uhhh, that's a G, brother," he'd say. Herlin Riley, who eventually replaced "Tain" Watts on the drums, says it still messes him up when he thinks about how J could retain all of that information so quickly and completely.

Then there are his powers of observation and ability to discern things around him. It was the damnedest thing. We would be in the greenroom and four women would walk in. He would sit and listen to the conversation, and when they walked out again he could describe every one of them: "Now, the fine one was the third one. The second one is heavy-set. The third one, I think she wore glasses." We couldn't believe it: "How does he know? How does a blind person know whether someone has some damned glasses on?" He would explain how he deduced things. "Well, the fine one, she spoke only a couple of sentences, but you all were deferring to her, and, based on the intelligence of what she said, she must have been fine."

For all his seriousness, Marcus is one of the funniest people in the world. Funny but precise. He believes in the supremacy of documentation. If you talked with him and used yourself as a reference, he'd say, "We started off discussing the economy. Now we're reduced to discussing you."

And we'd have heated discussions about everything. Who was greater, Beethoven or Bach? We had to bring in examples to back up our case. I was arguing for Beethoven so I brought in the Sixth Symphony. He was arguing for Bach so he would bring in all of *The Well-Tempered Clavier*, and we would go at it. I made a tape once of John

Coltrane's quartet and Beethoven's late string quartets, and we would listen to these things back and forth: "Man, listen to these four people playing." We talked about the effect of church music on improvisation; New Orleans polyphony; whether you could write fugues in the style of jazz; the value of arrangements vis-à-vis soloing; time changes; the meaning of being *modern;* football (we both love the Oakland Raiders); the quality of melodies; folk music. Once, in Seattle, we had a rare night off and we must have talked for nine or ten hours without stopping. That was twenty-three years ago, and even today when we see each other, we'll say, "Do you remember that conversation we had in Seattle?" We don't remember what we were talking about, but we damn sure were enjoying it.

Marcus *is* belief. He would say belief is the foundation of greatness, but you have to be able to access that belief to communicate with clarity and power in order to move people.

When he left the band in 1991, I can't tell you how I missed him. J is one of a kind in my generation. As far as I am concerned, he is the true innovator of our time. If you ask guys in the Jazz at Lincoln Center Orchestra to name who, of all the younger people they've played with, they consider a genius, they will always say Marcus and then tell some funny story about how he rehearsed them to death or gave them impossible-to-play music. They all respect and love him.

He has all the qualities necessary to be a great jazz musician: penetrating intelligence, an understanding of what's going on socially, the desire to make things better, knowledge of the blues, love of the tradition of the music, courage to take a stand, raw talent, discipline, a steadfast belief in himself, and endurance. He will not sacrifice his point of view. He doesn't mind playing different kinds of music, but he is going to play it the way he wants to play it.

Marcus has had to pay the price for his integrity. He didn't buckle under and he didn't have one of these big careers rooted in selling out, the way some guys have. He is still out there playing and swinging. His trio with Roland Guerin and my brother Jason on drums has a unique, contemporary sound. We recorded some music a couple of months ago, played some gigs, and gave some master classes, and after all these years, he has even more dedication. He is about playing, about the music, and about teaching. The J Master offers a stark contrast to a lot of what has gone on out here. He needs to be applauded and celebrated. Now. Marcus is for real.

Recommended Listening

Deep in the Shed
The Joy of Joplin
Blues for the New Millennium

In the spirit of swing: (from left) Marcus Printup, Walter Blanding, Ted Nash, and I parade through a houseful of people of all ages, colors, and kinds brought together—and lifted up—by jazz music.

CHAPTER SEVEN

That Thing with No Name

I've never understood why many consider creativity to be the mysterious province of some small, specialized group of people. Whenever I teach improvisation to young kids who are too shy to just go for whatever they can, I explain, "It's so easy. Just make up stuff. Yes, play anything that comes to mind, fingers, or lips. Louder! Wilder! That's it. You're improvising." After they produce a symphony of painful but free-spirited notes, I add, "I told you it was easy. It's only hard if you want to sound good."

Everywhere we look, we see the result of human creativity. I live in New York now, and it's mind-boggling just to think that every brick on every street, all of the glass, steel, and concrete, all of the art, signage, electrical wiring, plumbing, painting, and so on that makes Manhattan the most amazing metropolis in the world is someone's creation. The creativity of our fellow citizens is all around us—in their dress, language, lifestyle, in so many combinations of things. You don't have to earn your creativity—you're born with it. All you have to do is tend to it and unleash it. Every human being on earth is given the gift to create, and that creativity manifests itself in trillions of ways. There are no laws or rules. Creativity is unruly. Like a dream—you can't control what comes to you. You only control what portion you choose to tell.

How many times have we had off-the-wall ideas that someone else executes to tremendous success? How many times have we presented ideas that were laughed at? How many times have we come up with things that were actually dumb and deserved to be ridiculed? Some things stick and others don't.

But the mistakes can be helpful in developing a dynamic relationship with yourself. When you rise from some colossal failure or embarrassing miscalculation, you develop the thick epidermis required to present your creations to others. And you learn through practical experience the difference between theorizing and doing. Respect for your own creativity—what you are able to do and what you have been given the tools to accomplish—is a first step toward an unprecedented growth in personal productivity.

When I was beginning to play jazz around the world, critics and older musicians came out of the woodwork to say that my playing was inauthentic, lacked soul and feeling, and was too technical. In my young life, I had not paid enough dues to play with any meaning or feeling. This criticism rattled my confidence. I questioned my qualifications to play even though I suspected my life was as full of drama and strife as most people's, especially people my age. In my insecurity, I complained about this assessment of my playing to Sweets Edison, supreme master of blues trumpet.

He asked me, "Where are you from?"

I said, "New Orleans."

He said, "What did you grow up doing?"

I responded, "Playing."

"What did your daddy do?"

"Play."

Then he said, "What more do you want? Why are you trying to *act* like what you are? *Be* what you are." This was one of my most profound lessons about creativity—it's being yourself, valuing your own ideas, mining your own dreams.

This sounds simple enough, but in a world full of great ideas it's easy to get demoralized. After all, innovative ideas are often ridiculed, whereas old, traditional ideas may be accepted but are rarely celebrated. College jazz students almost always want to be innovators, people who change the world of the art form, like Louis Armstrong or Charlie Parker. Anything short of that is considered failure.

That's what I call the impossible standard, the Superman standard: The only thing that merits a youngster's study of jazz is the opportunity to redefine an art that he or she barely understands. Kids seek education for the chance to *be* one of the greats, not to learn from them. They don't consider the possibility that there could be something of substance in the music itself that merits study.

The writer Leonard Feather once asked Monk, "What about something new?"

Monk answered, "Let somebody else come up with something new. What about something good?"

The Superman standard is set so high you can't succeed. You will always feel that you are not doing enough. It's like being in a relationship with someone you can never make happy. The harder you try, the more you're accused of messing up.

When kids think innovation is the only way to be successful, unrealistic expectations prevent them from embracing the fundamentals of the art. It's as if they think listening to Charlie Parker will somehow compel them to play like him. (They don't need to worry; they won't.) If a musician doesn't love anything or want to be influenced by anything, he or she will never really experience the transcendent power of art. Believe it or not, some think that interacting with the music is like sleeping with the enemy, because its great achievements might influence their sound and sully their virginal, fresh concepts.

Kids tell me, "I want to move the art form forward." I tell them to get a stack of CDs, put them in a car, and take them from here to wherever they consider to be forward, because the art form is not going anywhere. You can make your contributions to it and they will be whatever they are. You will perhaps come up with some things that no one has come up with before, and those things will add beauty and substance to the art form. But you are not going to move it anywhere. It's like John Lewis used to say: "There's no next new movement. There never has been. There's just a beautiful broad mainstream." At the end of the day, Max Roach added a lot to a drum style that was already great; Jo Jones had played a lot of drums. Bud Powell played a pile of piano, but so had Art Tatum and James P. Johnson before him.

I always suggest youngsters consider the value of playing well, rather than worry about whether they will become another Thelonious Monk or Duke Ellington. There is power in achieving your personality and projecting it. The whole world may not imitate you, but you'll be satisfied. You have to play well before you can play great.

Someone can be creative inside or outside the mainstream of a tradition. Inside, you create new ways to do existing things better. Outside, you create a new world. Both options can be innovative. You can either reinvigorate a tradition or counterstate it. That's where knowledge of the arts can serve us all. The world of the arts presents examples of every imaginable type of person who has worked with *whatever he or she had* to make a cogent, powerful, and original statement. When we have knowledge of great innovators and understand their creativity, it can clear many roadblocks we believe affect only us. Their achievements educate, inspire, and delight.

Danny Barker taught us kids to respect the creativity and creative space of others. In that spirit, the second step toward growth in creative output is co-creation. Focus on what others can do and be flexible enough to adjust your thing to fit with theirs.

America is a young country. For all of our cockiness, we have suffered a crippling identity crisis. We spent many years under the illusion that the only valuable art was European. We also believed art exacerbated class distinctions. If you liked art you were a snob. Today, many of us still believe the arts to be some type of dreamy, nonessential, esoteric fluff. That's why they are always the first things cut from schools. The thought is that arts are impractical: "After all, most artists aren't paid anything much, if at all, and if they are paid it's for some type of vulgar desecration of sacred ideals." It's not necessary, like math or science. So goes the attack on public funding for the arts.

Some contemporary trends aside, art forms actualize the collective wisdom of a people. They represent our highest aspirations and our everyday ways, our concept of romance and our relationship to spiritual matters, as well as how we deal with birth, death, and everything in between. In short, the arts focus our identity and expand our awareness of the possible. They offer tools for survival with style in times of peace and war. If they are insightful, if they are well crafted, if they are accurate enough, they stand as testaments to the grandeur of a people across epochs. The achievements of Homer, Chaucer,

Michelangelo, Beethoven—important people from somewhere else and long ago—are part of the *lingua franca* of contemporary civilization.

Of all the arts created in America, jazz says the most about us. As democracy created an explosion of personal creativity, it stands to reason that the definitive art of America would have an unprecedented roll call of creative artists. To understand them and their achievements is to be armed with examples of creativity, courage, and endurance that would serve us all well.

But really, the most significant innovation is jazz itself. It tells us something about the importance of fulfilling a need. Art is created to nourish those who give birth to it. In the early 1800s, Beethoven said that in order to learn the truth of church music in his time, it was necessary to go back to the very earliest church modes. In other words, don't rely on conventional wisdom; go back to the original source.

I believe that to know the essence of a thing requires returning as closely as possible to the origin of that thing. The passage of time tends to quietly erode meaning and enthusiasm. The farther you move away from the sun, the colder it gets. The originators of jazz were only two generations removed from slavery. They were victims of rigorous forms of segregation that routinely and institutionally denied their humanity. So freedom was much more than a word to them. These pioneering musicians were exuberant about exhibiting this newfound personal freedom through their art. But they were also excited about hearing other people do the same thing. They understood that all were inextricably linked in freedom, just as they had been inextricably linked in bondage. And it wasn't theory; it was life as they lived it.

These originals were thrilled to share and communicate with all kinds of people. They became masters of achieving balance with others. Through improvising on the blues and tending to the collective rhythm that is swing, they worked out a perfect way to co-create. As we have seen, swing is both a rhythm that defined an era in American history and a worldview.

In this worldview, there is a belief in the power of collective decision making. Bad or mediocre decisions will be discarded or absorbed by the group in pursuit of a "better way" guided by feel and good taste. When a group of people working together feels something, when they trust that all are concerned for the common good, when they are determined to be in sync no matter what happens, that is swing—the feeling of " 'our way' *is* my way." This philosophy extends to how to treat audiences, consumers, staff, or even your family. It's not unrealistic. Just think about how whole congregations recite things in church every Sunday, almost together and completely unrehearsed. They proceed by feel.

On a jazz bandstand, swing is the single objective, the core that makes us all want to work together. Jazz—the music—is the collective aspirations of a group of musicians, shaped, given logic, and organized under the extreme pressure of time. When we all work together, the music swings, and when we don't, it doesn't. That's why, although the perception of jazz is that we all get along, in actuality, we're all always *trying* to get along. It is the integrity of that process that determines the quality of the swing.

This focus on perfecting the collective ebb and flow by clarifying intentions can be applied to any endeavor. A family that swings will be happier and much more successful. So will a business or a team. What you *intend* to do governs the assessment of action. That's why apologies are often simply, "That is not what I intended; I'm sorry." Presumably meaning, "My future actions will be much more in line with my true intent." Swing is pure intent made active. And it's valuable as a tool of diplomacy. With the new global technologies, cultures are coming closer and closer. As these cultures meet, tension and conflict seem to dominate our interactions. But, lest we confuse this friction with the end of the world, it's actually the *beginning* of the world, the Tower of Babel in reverse. We have been apart, now we are coming together: harmony through conflict.

To understand jazz, with its emphasis on personal creativity and responsibility to a collective, is to be better prepared to deal with the unprecedented global integration of our time. People with different belief systems aren't going to just go away. Everyone else is not going to abandon his or her way of life to be like us. And we are never going back to the good ol' *Ozzie and Harriet* 1950s, when everyone was in his and her "proper" place. It's time for a redefinition of citizenship that considers a world with far fewer boundaries.

As a boy, I was taught that our relationship to rights and responsibilities determines the quality of our citizenship. Generally, children are responsible only for themselves. As adults, we are responsible for more people—our families, our neighborhoods, our communities, our country, our world. It's an ever-expanding universe, and our ascension to a mature level of citizenship is directly related to the size and number of things we choose to take on.

In the arts, this ladder rises from your personal artistry to your art form, then on to all the arts, and finally to humanity itself.

Jazz insists on the undisputed sovereignty of the human being. In this technological era we can easily be fooled into believing that sophisticated machines are more important than progressive humanity. That's why art is an important barometer of identity. The arts let us know who we are in all of our glory, reveal the best of who we are. All the political and financial might in the world is diminished when put to the service of an impoverished cultural agenda. We see it in our schools, in our homes, and in our world profile: rich and fat, lazy and morally corrupt, with wild, out-of-control young people.

We all know that civilization requires a supreme effort. Our technology will become outmoded, but the technology of the human soul does not change. We still read Homer, but we're not that interested in using ancient Greek technology. We're not interested in returning to the aristocratic governments of Beethoven's time, but we still listen to his music because it still speaks to the depths of the human soul. He spelled it out for us in the Ninth Symphony. His music in its original form lifts our souls, today, right now. And while people in each era believe their times to be the worst times ever, there is always much to celebrate as well.

Jazz music reconciles opposites. It was created by the descendants of slaves but speaks eloquently of freedom. The blues—the lifeblood of jazz—ofttimes has heartbreaking melodies and lyrics set to a happy, dancing beat. But don't let the beat fool you. This is practical stuff. It keeps us rooted. And jazz can help us answer the cultural questions of our times: How can we use the aesthetic tools we have created to balance our lives? How do we address the technological advancements that make life softer without allowing them to eventually replace human interaction? How do we integrate with other cultures without disrespecting them or surrendering the best of what we are?

Jazz is the most flexible art form ever because it believes in the good taste of individuals. It believes in our ability to make reasonable choices. It takes a chance on our decision-making skills instead of legislating our freedom away with written restrictions and restrictive hierarchies. In jazz, the size of your heart and your ability to play determine your position in the band. The philosophy of jazz is rooted in the elevation and enrichment of people, plain ol' folks.

Respect and trust: These are the things jazz teaches. When you listen to great musicians, you hear the respect they have for one another's abilities; after all, rhythm section excluded, musicians always spend more time listening than playing. And, rhythm section *included*, you see the trust they have for one another because they are always making adjustments in response to what someone else has just created. I think Elvin Jones articulated it best when he said that in order to play with somebody on a profound level you have to be willing to die with him. Now, I'm not telling you to take that literally, but that is jazz, and that is true feeling at its most real.

In the simplest and most essential context, creativity and innovation reiterate the importance of soul. They are, separately and together, an expansion of feeling and a supreme expression of our humanity. We have an artistic imperative to understand and reengage creativity and innovation, not merely as tools for economic growth but as tools for democracy and accomplished citizenship. We have a cultural imperative to find common ground with even our fiercest competitors . . . and to play with integrity.

Perhaps the greatest lesson to be learned about integrity comes from the post–rock-and-roll era, when many jazz musicians decided to go commercial. The best jazz had always been the embodiment of integrity and conviction. Because the musicians' skills and competence were so hard-earned, it was difficult to get them to compromise. Once jazzmen began making the decision to water down their artistry for notoriety, publicity, or money, our art began to face the same challenges that our government and many businesses face: dearth of leadership, lack of quality, loss of meaning, insensitivity to people—ultimately a wholesale loss of faith: "Well, what is jazz, anyway?" "What difference does what I play make?"

But even in these fallow periods, all kinds of interesting things still take place. Our desire to testify through some type of art is unstoppable. A palpable energy is released when inspiration and dedication come together in a creative art. That energy is transformative in an individual who is innovative, but it is transcendent when manifested by a group. There are no words for the dynamic thrill of participating in a mutual mosaic of creativity. Remember, you don't have to earn your creativity—you were born with it. We are all potential artists, and artists cultivate their creativity obsessively, compelled by the need to create the feeling of community anywhere they can—in the subway, at a picnic, after dinner, even at a business convention. The feeling of giving enjoyment and enlightenment to the same human beings you have taken inspiration from is addictive.

It is that feeling that made the seventy-year-old Louis Armstrong, in the shadow of death, lips as scarred as the moon, reach for those last blood-soaked notes. That feeling made sickly, deaf Beethoven wake up and press his head against the soundboard of a piano at 2:37 A.M. to reassess a troublesome passage in a supreme masterpiece that still speaks to us almost two hundred years later. That feeling made old, bedridden Henri Matisse strain with a long stick to place figures on the ceiling by memory and feel, after becoming almost blind from years of working with too-intense colors. It made Duke Ellington, after fifty years on the road and with only months to live, ravenously listen to his band play as many of their two thousand pieces as possible, gorging himself on a last glorious meal of what they had done with their lives. These masters didn't want it to stop. Ever.

That thing with no name. It's what some tired, old cowboy with a harmonica played and sang to survive a hard cattle drive and some bad coffee. It's what we all want to feel and be a part of. It's our birthright. We just don't know it. But if we listen to the great artists of history, many of whom lived in times much more difficult than ours, they tell us that this explosion of consensual creativity is not only here and now and always, it's the only thing worth our energy and resources and time.

In the words of Duke Ellington, "*The* people *are* my people." When we accept that credo as our own, then we will rise above the disappointments of the past and make real the dreams of our ancestors. I can still hear the words of Danny Barker: "Now, that's jazz."

Wynton Marsalis and Justice Sandra Day O'Connor discussed jazz and the Constitution during "Let Freedom Swing: A Celebration of America."

AFTERWORD

A Conversation Between Wynton Marsalis and Justice Sandra Day O'Connor

At the Kennedy Center celebration called "Let Freedom Swing: A Celebration of America," held in Washington, D.C. on the eve of Barack Obama's inauguration as forty-fourth president of the United States, Supreme Court Justice Sandra Day O'Connor and Wynton Marsalis had a conversation about jazz and the Constitution that was inspired by *Moving to Higher Ground*. The following is an excerpt.

Wynton Marsalis: One of the beautiful things about jazz improvisation is that you can take something that we all know and you can make it into another piece that still keeps its identity. It's like how the Constitution can be amended. It's still the same Constitution, but here's our take on it. That means it is always new because the ideals are valid, they're timeless.

Sandra Day O'Connor: I like the way, in the book, you related what happens in a good jazz band with what happens in a good democracy.

WM: I think that that's what the Constitution is, a collection of virtuosos who got together and they grappled with problems.

SDOC: The great contribution the framers of our Constitution made was developing the form of our government, three separate branches—the presidency, the legislative branch, and the judicial branch—giving each one some powers over the other two.

WM: And they worked through those problems by a delicate way of balancing individual rights, the rights of states, what is the central government's role—and in music we do that all the time. The drummer is like the president, the loudest instrument.

SDOC: Is that the president, the drums?

WM: Yes, the drum is the president.

SDOC: Okay. What's the bass then? That's pretty loud too.

WM: The judiciary.

SDOC: Oh, the judicial branch.

WM: There's a great bass player named Milt Hinton. He's called The Judge.

SDOC: He keeps them steady.

WM: He addresses the harmony and the rhythm. And he's in the center of the rhythm section, so he's in the central location where he can understand everything that's going on, has an influence on the ground rhythm and on the harmony. But the piano in the rhythm section would be like the legislative branch. The piano represents all of the notes, all of the keys.

SDOC: The piano can play everything. And you have to listen to each other. I mean that's the point. When one of you is playing a solo, the others play along, but they listen.

WM: One of the greatest lessons on the bandstand is that you're forced to listen to everybody else, so it teaches you to be open in your hearing.

SDOC: Well now if we can just get members of the legislative branches to pay a little more attention to the theory of jazz music, we'll all be a little better off. Do you think?

WM: I'm with you.

SDOC: I like this passage in the book where you say, "When a group of people working together feel something, when they trust that all are concerned for the common good, when they're determined to be in sync no matter what happens, that is swing."

WM: Swing is a matter of equilibrium. The Constitution is a supreme example of swing. How can we figure out how to meet each other's objectives and be together and for it to feel good? Now, when we look at swing, it brings together opposites. So let's take the bass for example. When we amplify the softest instrument and also the lowest, the bass is forced to play on every beat with the cymbal, which as a part of the drum set is the loudest instrument and the highest-pitched. When they get along and they work it out, you have a great time. When they don't, you got a long night. The musicians are always saying, "We're doing our best when we play together, we're going to play this tune, we're going to come together, and we are together."

SDOC: I think maybe our country in this recent election has come together in a way that holds some promise for the future.

WM: We are invigorated—the whole world is uplifted by this decision.

SDOC: Well, we all wish this new government the very best, don't we? We want it to succeed.

WM: Yes. And we're going to help it to succeed.

Index

Page numbers in italics indicate photo captions.

Danny Barker's band in 1970: I'm wearing the striped high-water pants; to my left is Herlin Riley.

ABOUT THE AUTHORS

WYNTON MARSALIS was born in New Orleans and studied with Art Blakey and the Jazz Messengers. He is now the artistic director of Jazz at Lincoln Center and has won many awards, significant and trivial.

GEOFFREY C. WARD is the author of *Jazz: A History of America's Music; The War;* and many other books.

Both Marsalis and Ward are members of the celebrated Serengeti Club.